MY HANDS, REMEMBERING

a memoir by **Lauren Fath**

Passengers Press 2022

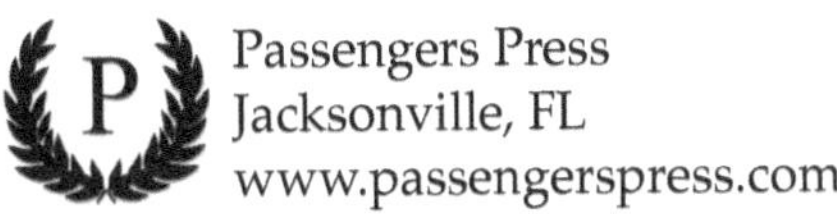

Passengers Press
Jacksonville, FL
www.passengerspress.com

Fath, Lauren
1st edition.
ISBN: 979-8-218-05247-8

Manuscript Editor: Femi Sobowale
Press Editor-in-chief: Zac Furlough

Author photograph: Kerry Kehoe
Cover design and book layout: Andreea Ceplinschi

For my grandma,

Evelyn Louise (Kelley) Fath

November 15, 1922 – September 22, 2011

CONTENTS

HAYSTACKS

Columbia, Missouri, 2010

When my husband and I moved to our Missouri town, into our small, white house in late summer of 2010, his towering upright bass became the centerpiece of our living room. It leaned in a corner by day, but come dark, Pete would pull it to the center of the room and play for hours. I reveled in the moments when Bach's cello suites, transposed an octave lower, hummed through the air. Pete's bow slid over the strings, and his long, sturdy fingers lingered in soft vibrato on the instrument's neck. Pete called the bass his "dancing partner," and he played it like its nickname. He leaned his hip into the cut-out curve of its side, hovered over it protectively, wrapped his arm around it in search of low, far-down notes. Its somber resonance rang through our rooms, as if to color everything the same sepia as the instrument's varnished skin. Pete played with the windows open while I sat on the front porch—which wasn't really a porch, but rather, a humble slab of concrete. I listened to his notes flow into the soft night and up, up, up, as if to be illuminated by the moon.

But by the next summer, Pete had left. He had left me for another woman, for another city, taking with him the upright bass, its somber notes in the night. Thirty-one years old and just two years married, then, I lived alone in the small, white house. Still, fireflies dotted the lawn at dusk, and still, violent July storms shook tree limbs to the roof, and the summer humidity sat wet on my skin. Still, I sat mostly on the front porch, because inside it was too quiet.

* * *

Change began in late March, as I finished the first year of my PhD program, when Pete, an architect by training, got a call from a firm in our hometown of Chicago. One of his former bosses was now a principal there. They were swamped, the old boss told him, and they needed someone to come to town for a two-month project. It would begin the next week. Pete and I cheered at this news, and each of us took a whiskey shot at the bar where we were watching an afternoon Cubs game on TV.

"You have to go," I said.

I'm sure he thought I would react differently, would tell him not to go. But it was clear he hadn't been happy in our small city, where he'd been working at an organic grocery and piecing together gigs with a couple of jazz trios. Pete's heart, I knew, was still in the "City of the Big Shoulders," as Carl Sandburg called it—though at the time I didn't know the extent of his reasons. I knew that any high-rise architect would be discontent in a city whose tallest downtown building was a ten-story hotel and its newest, a concrete parking garage. But I kept telling myself he would, eventually, adjust to our new life, though I now see that I didn't do enough to help his adjustment. In fact, I did the opposite: I poured myself into schoolwork, spending long days in class and teaching, then coming home only to hunker down in my office. Pete cooked dinner and kept the house clean, and I wonder how often I thanked him. I'm certain it wasn't often enough. Now, however, I suspect that Pete was not only unhappy with the city or with me; he was unhappy for the burdensome secret he was harboring.

After Pete had been back in Chicago six weeks, on a Monday in early May, we were messaging online because he had lost his cell phone. Over Google chat, he told me about the affair. It was with our friend Veronica, also an architect in Chicago. It had been intermittent for a year, he said, its incidents rather humble (flirting, kissing) and not begging anything more dangerous. After all, he had moved to Missouri with me after the affair began, so its brief opportunities to burgeon were limited to our holiday returns home. But since his return to Chicago, he and Veronica had been together quickly, recklessly.

"What has happened between the two of you?" I typed, wanting to know just how quickly, how recklessly.

"Everything," he replied.

And the next two days have disappeared. I remember everything as if it's underwater, distorted and blue-hued. I remember sitting on my front porch, watching turquoise light then indigo dusk then navy-black dark wash over my lawn. I remember waking at five in the morning and stumbling aimlessly around the still-dim house, convinced that I had not actually awakened, that none of this could be real.

* * *

I suspected Pete's affair at least a couple of weeks before he told me. We talked on the phone nightly, but each time, he seemed more distant, distracted, terse. I called him one Saturday night, and hearing bar noise in the background, asked where he was.

"With Veronica," he answered, "at a birthday party for one of her friends. I'll step outside." At the time, his being out with her was hardly cause for alarm. She was a mutual friend of ours, and I knew she lived close to the apartment Pete was subletting for his short stay.

"Do you have a few minutes to talk?" I asked, hearing the Chicago wind whisper into his phone's receiver.

"Not really," he said. "I've got things to do."

It was not the answer I'd expected, and my lower lip quivered. I'm not sure what prompted me to ask him, but I did: "What's wrong, Pete? Are you seeing someone?"

"Just seeing friends," he answered, and then repeated it as if to assure himself—"Just friends." And then he hung up.

A week or so later, Veronica posted a photo album on Facebook of a party she and Pete had both attended. Pete was in nearly all of the photos. They were reverent, capturing his wide grin, his head-thrown-back laugh, the way he really listens to people when they're talking. I witnessed the beauty I saw in him, the love I had for him, through someone else's eyes, and I knew that type of seeing was reserved for those in love.

Maybe I should have suspected even earlier. After the first semester of my PhD program, Pete and I returned to Chicago for Christmas break. One night, we met up with a group of friends at our local bar, the one where we'd always gathered to watch Bears games, the one whose bartender and other patrons we referred to as our "second family." I was sitting at the bar, talking to friends. Pete and Veronica were in the small back room, playing pool. For some reason, I stood up and looked back toward the pool table. There, leaned in close against a wood-paneled wall, I swore I saw him kiss her. They were standing too close, their pool cues propped in a corner. When I asked Pete about it, he told me I'd been imagining things, that I needed to trust him, that I was just jealous. Knowing my own proclivity for distrust, I convinced myself all of these were true.

* * *

In our ten-year relationship, I'd always had trouble trusting Pete. I blamed my wariness on our several breakups and reunions, which began when we were undergraduates and ended on that Monday in early May—I thought at the time. We had, of course, ended long before.

One summer, when we knew I'd be moving soon for my two-year master's program in Oregon, we had agreed to stop being exclusive. Pete would remain in Chicago to finish his own master's degree in architecture. We were still seeing each other, though, still spending nights curled together in the center of a bed. Once, when we were almost asleep, I don't know what compelled me to ask him, but I did: "Who's the last person you were with who wasn't me?"

He answered with the name of someone I'd encountered at occasional gatherings, though I wouldn't have called her a friend.

"When?" I replied, surprised.

"Last weekend," he said.

"What happened between the two of you?"

"I don't remember. I was drunk. But I woke up with my clothes on."

I got out of bed, went out to my back porch, and sat drinking a beer I didn't want. Eventually, he came out and sat down with me. He offered to leave.

"No, stay," I said. And he did. Years later, when we were already

12

married, I asked again about that night. He told me he did remember what happened. He told me what had happened. It was just shy of everything.

"Why didn't you tell me when I asked?"

"I was afraid," he said.

The lie from years before had been enough to fracture my trust, to leave us slightly less intact. I wondered constantly what else he wasn't telling me because I hadn't asked.

In May, after I did, at last, ask—"What has happened between the two of you?"—he told me: He had been kissing Veronica that December night by the pool table. He had been kissing her since the summer before we left Chicago—kisses stolen at bars while I taught evening classes, kisses stolen at the ends of long nights when he walked her home, even kisses, he told me, stolen at our going-away party, in the kitchen, while I was out on our back porch opening beer bottles for guests and posing, wide-smiled, for photos.

* * *

After Pete told me, after two days awash in blue, I took the bus to Chicago. He couldn't meet up until evening, after work. That left me the afternoon to stroll the Loop streets, their gray, looming skyscrapers and shadowed sidewalks still familiar. I took refuge in the anonymity of the large city, in the din of the elevated train, the dirge of slow-moving traffic, the low hum that crept up through sidewalk grates—as if all these could drown out my despair. I liked that my own worries seemed small amid the urban dissonance, whereas they had been too large for my silent Missouri house.

Pete and I used to have an annual tradition of taking a day off work, each fall, to visit the Art Institute of Chicago. I liked the Modern

Wing best—the Rothkos and Magrittes—but always, after visiting that and the basement photography exhibits, we would make our way up the curvaceous marble staircase to the Impressionists. Pete always lingered longest before Monet's *Haystacks*, six paintings that show stacks of hay in a field at the end of harvest season, each lambent in a different-colored light cast from the sky—yellow morning, burning orange as the sun falls, bruised blue of near-night. I never held these stacks of hay in much regard.

"Why," I always asked Pete, "would someone paint the same thing over and over again?" In fact, I didn't at the time know the extent of Monet's persistence: For those displayed in Chicago are just six in a series of twenty-five.

Even though, on this afternoon, it was early summer and not fall—the sun a bit too high in the sky, the sidewalks shimmering with heat—the Art Institute seemed to pull me in. More specifically, I felt the haystacks, by their own quiet force, urging me inside. I skipped the Modern Wing, skipped the photography—and how large those marble stairs are, up to the Impressionists, when one is alone. Perhaps that recognition of my aloneness—not just in the moment, but now, permanently—was what allowed me this:

I stood for too long before the haystacks. I wept.

I had always seen them as indicative of artistic stasis, of Monet's being stuck in a rut and able to paint just one thing. But I now see that the reason I was drawn to that series, on that day, was not the emotional significance it held—the works were, after all, the ones Pete always gazed at the longest while I grew bored beside him. Rather, I saw then what Monet had done: He had painted the change happening around him, change that was beyond his control but perceptible in how the light on that hay glowed less brightly, how the cover on the ground grew thinner by winter. Yes, Monet had, in each painting, frozen one moment in the progression of change, had seen the inevitability of life's movement and attempted to encapsulate moments on that spectrum, to freeze them. By capturing moments that will cease to be, we immortalize them, in a way. We can look back nostalgically on what we've captured, and while we know that it no longer is, we can still hold on to it by our having made it into art.

I urged myself, in that moment, not to forget the progression of my own change. I urged myself not to forget how, in our first apartment together, the sun came at late afternoon through our west-facing living room windows and lay in slanted lines across an orange rug. I urged myself not to forget how, in our Ukrainian Village apartment years later, the bedroom light was largely blocked by a building next door, so mornings were rendered a dusty, pale blue-gray that crept across Pete's face as he slept. And I urged myself not to forget how, in a blizzard that kept us indoors for days during our only Missouri winter together, the sun's reflection on glistening snow lit our small, white house the brightest it had ever been—so bright we pulled down the blinds and made love. All of these, now, are immortalized. That is art: It is the place where what is lost and what is preserved are the same. It is the paradox that warns us against forgetting.

* * *

Pete and I met up in the Bucktown neighborhood, at dusk. We circled the neighborhood blocks, unsure where to go. Finally, we sat on a bench in front of an elementary school, the sun going down behind us, the pastel sky darkening.

"Why didn't you tell me this earlier?" I asked.

"Because I was afraid," he said. "I was afraid of hurting you."

I told him I wanted to work it out. I was willing to forgive him. I already had, I said, though I'm not sure I believed myself.

"Let's fix this," I urged, begging.

"This is unfixable," he replied. "Lauren, I don't love you anymore."

I still wonder whether he believed this, or whether he had convinced himself it was true. After all, the next day we met up for lunch at an old favorite restaurant near where I was staying with friends. It was raining outside as we walked there, a cold, driving rain that put winter back in the air. I removed my wet sweater but shivered as we took seats at the bar. Pete placed his sweatshirt over my shoulders, the smell of talc and sweat a reminder of sleeping beside him.

As we ate, I struggled not to instinctively reach over and put my hand on his knee, the way I always had. It felt like such a natural gesture, so hard to suppress after so many years. He accidentally called me "honey," then apologized quickly—to me or to himself, I'm not sure.

After lunch, we walked around the neighborhood, called "Printer's Row" for its history as the city's publishing center. We stopped into a used bookstore and paged together through large books of architecture photos, through the poetry of Mark Strand. It felt like we were us again, though his voice was softer when he spoke, his laugh less frequent, his eyes downcast. I tried to forget that he was leaving me—that he had already left me—a stubborn, deliberate forgetfulness I still have not overcome, though now, days go by that I do not think of him.

* * *

"We tell ourselves stories in order to live," Joan Didion begins her essay collection *The White Album*. "We live entirely, especially if we are writers, by the imposition of a narrative line upon disparate images, by the 'ideas' with which we have learned to freeze the shifting phantasmagoria which is our actual experience." Now, my mind divides time into before-knowing and after-knowing. Now I see that no narrative I impose upon my life can, in fact, freeze it. We cannot go back and change what we thought was true. Narrative documents the truth as we knew it, not what continues to be true. What is true, now, is this: Pete and I divorced less than six months after that Chicago visit. Shortly before our court date, in September 2011, I wrote to him about Monet's haystacks, likening them to our impending split. His response was this:

To me, the haystacks have always seemed hollow. Like if Monet were to paint from a slightly different angle, we would see a door and a hearth inside. Perhaps I'm looking to see permanence in those paintings . . . but they always just seem so light. Because I know that if they were hollow (sheltering us) they would definitively blow away.

As such, hollow or not, blown away or not, the farmer would still bundle them next season. So what then is the truth? Is there a door on the other side with a kettle on the fire? Are they frozen solid 'til spring? Couldn't it be both?

The only truth about them is that they were painted. "Frozen," as you say. One cannot apply present knowledge on the past and change its narrative. The narrative is fixed, perspective is not. Whether or not you can see the door is up to you.

* * *

My old truths, then, are haystacks dismantled, bundled, carted away after harvest. They are low bass notes dissipating in thick summer humidity. Neither can remain. But I'm beginning to think nothing true can stay that way forever—not even the pull of planets, not the moon's orbit around the place we all call home, not the now-silent porches we sit on by night, still looking up, up, up.

METRONOME

Columbia, Missouri, 2010

Pete and I had moved to Missouri on August 1, 2010, giving ourselves about two weeks to unpack and get settled before I began school. Even before we set out, our move had been fraught with small calamities. The day before, in Chicago, when we had arrived at the rental office to claim our empty moving truck, we were told that all the trucks had already been rented out, so despite our reservation, which I'd made months in advance, we would have to wait for someone else to return a truck. Pete and I and a few of our friends—who should have been helping us move furniture by this time—took turns camping out on a picnic blanket in front of the rental office, a sad, cinder-block shanty under the ramp where Interstate 94 funnels cars onto Milwaukee Avenue, just a mile or so from the apartment we were eager to pack up and leave. Pete brought me lunch from a nearby sandwich shop, and I brought him coffee. I spent my time sitting in front of the office silently seething, and then deciding to do something about it. I called other rental agencies in Chicago, but they, too, were truck-less. It was, after all, the most popular time to move: the end of the month in the middle of summer. Soon, our friends had given up hope and gone home. Pete and I were, by then, surrounded by an increasing number of desperate strangers, all of whom attempted to argue with the unapologetic woman behind the counter before joining us on the concrete outside.

Around seven in the evening, when the nearby highway noise had quieted and the sun was sinking lower in the sky, when all the others had left and Pete and I were the only two remaining, when even the rental office had closed, the clerk instructing us—if a truck were returned—to sign a piece of paper and slip it through a mail slot, two people pulled up in a truck. We returned to our apartment, victorious but already exhausted, and called all our friends back over to help us load the large items: our sofa, bed, heavy boxes full of kitchen appliances. Pete and I stayed up late into the night, after everyone else had left, loading smaller boxes and packing up the last loose items. We argued over whether to pack half-eaten containers of food. Pete wanted to bring them along. But space was getting tight in the truck, I said. These last few scoops of peanut butter weren't worth the room they'd take up. My attitude surprised me: I was normally the less wasteful one of us, reluctant to throw things out, washing and re-using Ziploc bags, purchasing items like Tupperware at thrift stores, where they were abundant for fifty cents. I don't remember, now, whether we brought along the peanut butter or not. It's beside the point, I suppose, to revisit how small arguments ended when a much larger ending—though I didn't know it at the time—was just around the corner. But I saw these small arguments as innocuous spats, not as a symptom of what they were: problems far deeper than peanut butter, even with our new life on the horizon.

The trip from Chicago to Columbia, Missouri, was seven hours. I drove Pete's Honda Civic with the upright bass—our most precious cargo—reclining in the passenger seat next to me. Pete trailed behind in the hard-won rental truck. We had signed the lease on our new Missouri house sight unseen, faxing papers back and forth with the landlord. We'd inherited it from an outgoing graduate student and her boyfriend, so we'd figured it couldn't be half-bad. When we arrived, the landlord gave us the keys and a brief lesson on how to start the fickle lawnmower that came with the house. At the time, I was thrilled by the prospect of having a lawn to mow, not at all aware of how quickly grass and weeds would overwhelm me in the hot, humid summers of the Missouri River Valley. Everything, at this point—even yard work—was tinged with an aura of novelty and industrious possibility. I felt that we were pioneers, embarking on our own modern-day westward journey. Pete and I both knew we were sacrificing our city life for what we saw, at the time, as Missouri's simplicity. We were eager to embrace small-town life, to shop and eat locally, to strip our lives of expensive rent and daily subway commutes, crowded sidewalks and the constant thrum of traffic. Perhaps this search for simplicity is best reflected by the fact that, while we were getting settled, I chose to spend my evenings re-reading Laura Ingalls Wilder's *The Little House on the Prairie*. I'd loved the book as a child, and something in me wanted to return to its idealism, as if my Missouri life might shape up the same way as Laura's had: "Softly Pa's fiddle sang in the starlight. Sometimes he sang a little and sometimes the fiddle sang alone. Sweet and thin and far away, the fiddle went on singing: 'None knew thee but to love thee, / Thou dear one of my heart . . . ' The large, bright stars hung down from the sky. Lower and lower they came, quivering with music." The next day, after the singing stars have receded into the daylight and the wagon has traveled farther, Pa Ingalls announces, "Here we are, Caroline! Right here we'll build our house."

Pete and I, too, felt we had arrived when we pulled up in front of our small, white Missouri house, which was nothing special: a square, single-story house divided into quadrants—at the front, the living room and a space I'd call my office; in the back, the kitchen, bedroom, and bathroom. A porch leading to the backyard had been enclosed and converted into a laundry room, replete with even more finicky, old appliances we never would quite figure out. The house was, for the most part, stark and sterile, its walls painted flat white and the carpet a dull ivory, like old piano keys. Its one attempt at charm was in the kitchen, whose walls were papered floor to ceiling in a mauve and gray-blue print of hearts and filigree. The same hearts and filigree had been stenciled in acrylic paint on the cabinet doors. Pete and I would quickly cover up the stenciling by taping vintage photographs and posters over it, but the wallpaper was inescapable. To its credit, the house had abundant kitchen counter space, two large closets in the bedroom, and plenty of windows that filled it with light—luxuries seldom afforded by city living.

Even after we'd unloaded our furniture into the house, it still felt too large, too empty. In time, we would grow accustomed to the extra space, the room to move around each other, a separateness we'd not been allowed in our Chicago apartment. At this point, on this first day, we still gravitated to the same rooms at the same time. After it had grown dark, we sat on stools in the kitchen, listening to Leonard Cohen and staring at opened boxes of newspaper-wrapped plates and glasses. As we sized up our next task, a huge cockroach—the length of my pinky finger—scuttled across the linoleum floor and lodged itself beneath one of our boxes. Pete moved the box aside and stepped on the bug, which made a loud crunch beneath his sneaker. Were there more? we wondered aloud. Or was this a fluke, a bug that had come through the open door as we'd moved in? We convinced ourselves that we didn't have a cockroach problem. I would later learn that the word "cockroach" is an English corruption of the Spanish *cucaracha*, which means "loathsome bug." The presence of cockroaches in a dream indicates the exposure of problems that have remained hidden: What has been suppressed until now crawls, as the bug does, out of hiding.

* * *

Our move to Missouri had felt like the fulfillment of something, maybe of wanderlust, which we finally were able to enact together—as if it would fix us. I am reminded of a Dana Gioia poem called "Summer Storm," which ends with these lines:

> *There are so many* might have beens,
> What ifs *that won't stay buried,*
> *Other cities, other jobs,*
> *Strangers we might have married.*
>
> *And memory insists on pining*
> *For places it never went,*
> *As if life would be happier*
> *Just by being different.*

Happier by being different: That was, I know now, what we thought we would be. But Missouri only made us both more miserable, or perhaps I should say more miserable together. Individually, we were happy. Problem was, we were two people living separately in the same home, trying to hide our latent desires.

It wasn't that way, at first. I hadn't yet started school, and Pete was jobless. Mornings, we woke up early, the bedroom flooded with sun and heat, the cool nighttime air giving way, temperatures topping a hundred degrees. We made the twenty-minute walk from our house to the city's small downtown, where Pete would buy iced coffee and I, iced tea. We window-shopped in front of still-closed stores and picked up free local magazines from boxes on the street, trying to figure out what the town had in store for us. At midday, the heat no longer bearable, we returned home and lazed in the air conditioning. Eager for fall, I had begun knitting a sweater—a simple pullover in beige wool. Pete returned to the upright bass with a vigor I'd not seen in months, spending hours each day playing scales in time with his electronic metronome. It is that metronome whose sound I remember most from those first Missouri days—not the whir of the window air-conditioning unit or the brush of Pete's horsehair bow against bass strings, but the quiet, steady tick-tock, the simulated sound of a mallet on a wooden block, holding together our daily rhythm.

After a week, we decided to start a garden, or rather, I decided. I was inexperienced but persistent, undeterred by my failed attempt, the summer earlier, at urban gardening. It wasn't that I'd failed in the traditional sense, however: In our small Chicago backyard, in a narrow strip of landscaping that abutted the lawn, I had selected a two-by-two-foot area that was in the sun for at least half the day, and for some reason, I decided cucumbers would be my crop. The cucumbers had grown wildly, in spite of the sullied soil, from which I'd dug up a beer bottle and countless other glass shards while planting the seeds. Cucumbers have a trailing habit, our neighbor Liz told me. But even with Liz's advice, I was not at all prepared for just how much these cucumbers would "trail." They trailed out of the strip of landscaping and, at first, a few feet onto the porch outside our back door. Within a month, they had overtaken the porch, so that we had to step over the vines as we entered or left.

When the first of the cucumbers was big enough to pick, I plucked it from its thick stem and brought it inside. Pete lingered behind me as I placed it on the cutting board and cut off one end, then made two thick slices, one for each of us. The flavor was delicately sweet, the flesh robust and juicy. It was a good cucumber, but at that moment, I regretted my decision: I don't really like cucumbers. In fact, I often pick them off restaurant salads and lay them to the side. We put the rest in a plastic bag, where it languished in the back of the fridge until one of us threw it away.

This time, in Missouri, Pete humored me again, and we found our way to a garden center just up the road. We bought canvas gloves and a fifty-foot hose, a sprinkler head for the hose, a spade with a retractable handle, and seeds for green beans, zucchini, kale, and broccoli. Little did we know that the summer of 2010 would turn out to be the hottest since 1980 for Missouri.

Back home, the first task at hand was to bring the lawn and weeds under control. I retrieved the lawnmower from our garage, which was useless despite its designation: It housed the landlord's woodworking equipment, old rainwater barrels, and furniture apparently left by previous tenants, warped by humidity and time. I pulled the lawnmower through the back gate and tugged at its stubborn starter cord, stabilizing it with one leg propped against the motor. It sputtered and spat black smoke, but I could tell the blade was turning, because twigs and rocks shot out from beneath the mower deck. I began making laps in the grass, reveling in the industry of so simple a task. When I approached the back porch, I mowed closely along the stairs, careful to catch the weeds growing between seams in the concrete. At one turn, I saw a small, black head—a snake—peer out from a hole in the steps. As I rounded the mower around the next corner, careful to stay flush with the house, I was suddenly surrounded by snakes, black and yellow striped, slinking between my sneakers, moving in a frenzy to escape. Some were caught beneath the blade, a bloody pulp before I could jump back, killing the mower's engine when I let go of the handle. I confess I didn't feel bad. I'd heard of Missouri's snakes: copperheads and rattlers and water moccasins, and I couldn't have known one type from the other. These were mere garter snakes, and I would come to learn that they'd made a home in the slim space between the back porch and the house—a small, dark, and damp cavern for spending these hot, sunny days. The snakes were harmless, I knew, but after my encounter, I became afraid to use the back door—afraid to hang laundry on the line or water the lawn—because I knew the snakes lay coiled just out of sight, an invisible threat not unlike the one lurking beneath my own marriage.

Nonetheless, I continued my pursuit of an idyllic backyard. I climbed up on a stepladder and tore down vines from the side of the house—honeyvine milkweed, a notorious Missouri pest, which had suctioned itself to the wood siding. Its broad, heart-shaped leaves had grown in droves, stems winding through the chain-link fence and up gutters, swathing the north side of the house. I tugged at the unrelenting vines until they gave, then clipped the remnants from the fence with scissors, lacking any proper tool. Pete and I dug the roots of the vines from the front landscaping, where they'd started, stabilizing themselves on an electrical meter planted in the soil. We dug with the humble spade, taking turns going deeper and deeper, sawing through roots so thick they looked more like tree trunks. When the area was free of weeds, Pete "tilled" it with a metal rake he'd found in the garage, several of its tines missing or bent. We planted the seeds—vegetables on one side of the front door, flowers on the other. And then we watered and waited.

School began for me, and I suspect Pete found himself bored, sitting home alone all day. Before long, he had signed on as a volunteer at Habitat for Humanity, where he helped build houses on weekends, and he'd also taken a job at a local organic grocery called the Root Cellar. The grocery, especially, was a good deal for someone otherwise unemployed: He would work there one day a week, for eight hours, and get paid in groceries—eighty dollars' worth for a shift. On Tuesdays, after I'd finished with classes for the day, I would drop by the Root Cellar and meet Pete. We planned our meals for the week and picked out groceries, filling our tote bags with the ingredients that Pete, inevitably, would use to cook dinner. For with me a full-time graduate student again, Pete had taken over nearly all of our household responsibilities. After all, I told myself, I hated to cook and he loved it. I think he saw cooking as akin to jazz improvisation: He started with the recipe, but added extra ingredients like riffs on the bass, ending up with something that resembled what he'd set out to create, but that wasn't quite true to its intended form.

The best meal I remember, though, was one we collaborated on—an anomaly, for I would often come home to find dinner already in the works. But on this occasion, we worked together. The plan was ground lamb sliders and roasted sweet potato fries. I would make the buns from scratch, and Pete would handle the burgers and fries. While I'm a terrible cook, I can bake reasonably well, since I'm a stickler for following directions. While I kneaded the bread dough and set it aside to rise, I stopped to take a picture—which is still stored on my digital camera—of Pete on the back porch, crouched over our tiny kettle grill, flipping the burgers. The sun is going down behind him, and he looks golden, happy. That's how I like to remember him in that house, but I suppose it couldn't stay that way forever. Still, I've captured the moment, and doing so has shaped my memory of how things were, even if they were like that for just an instant. I also photographed the sliders. As usual, Pete had improvised: he had worked minced mint into the lamb meat, added Havarti cheese and arugula to top the burgers. They were delicious—savory and grilled just right, so they were crisp on the outside and tender inside.

But not all nights were like this one. I remember, as my course-work occupied more and more of my time, that I came to resent Pete's dinners. I didn't want to, didn't have time to, set aside my work for an hour and eat at the kitchen table. I felt a certain nagging impatience during our meals, one that made me silent and tense, disengaged from the conversation while I worked through Russian translations or short-story responses in my mind. I don't know why I didn't just talk to Pete about my work; he was as academic as I was, and even as interested in my work as I was. During our master's programs, we'd always shared what we learned, snail-mailing articles on architecture or literature back and forth across the country—Chicago to Oregon, Oregon to Chicago. But somehow, that sharing lost its appeal when we were in the same house. There wasn't the same romantic luster to handing texts back and forth over the dinner table, I suppose. And so I ate quickly and silently, without appreciation, and then returned to my office. I was beginning to feel that Pete and I had built our separate niches, not dependent on each other, but merely tolerant.

What if we were just two people who listened to Leonard Cohen and loved the idea of being together more than the thing, togetherness, itself? We both, I see now, subscribed to the notion that things could be better if only they could be different, a notion that moving to Missouri had nurtured and coddled. What we couldn't see was that nothing would change if we couldn't change ourselves—something I'm still not sure anyone can do, not wholly or completely, not in the ways we needed to change to stay together and be happy doing so. My distrust for Pete ran so deep that, in some ways, I wonder whether his affair was a self-fulfilling prophecy. Did he cheat because, for so many years, I had openly told him that I thought he would cheat? Was his affair, then, inevitable? Did I want it, just to prove myself right? Pete and I both brought a sort of wanderlust to our relationship, and it didn't end once we were married. We let our imaginations stray to other possibilities—mostly, the possibility of not being together at all.

* * *

Pete and I had established a routine, once a week, of meeting up after my evening writing workshop. Most often, we went to Ragtag—an indie cinema combined with a bakery, restaurant, and a bar. We would sometimes see a documentary, other times get dinner or drinks. One evening in late fall, we ran into my friend Carmen, a graduate student in another department, sitting at the bar and tapping away at her laptop. Pete and I took seats beside her. I confess, even with Pete right next to me, I felt the tinge of my crush on Carmen. She had the longest eyelashes, the best clothes, the most ringing laugh. Everything about her was superlative. So when, that night, after a couple of glasses of wine, she invited Pete and me to her house, I reveled quietly in the invitation, convinced Pete to stay out just a little longer. I confess, I wondered what would happen. I knew Carmen was bisexual, and we had, in the short time we'd known each other, gestured toward flirtation—a close leaning in on our barstools, a friendly "hello" hug extended just a shade too long.

I admired her for being able to identify as I didn't feel I could. I envied her for being able to act on all her desires, rather than to be confined to a singular one, as I was. But I was married, I told myself. I had what I wanted. Secure as I felt in the small, white house, I recognize now that I wanted something I couldn't have, so long as I was tethered to Pete. He, too, wanted something he couldn't have, so long as he was tethered to me. So was this, then, my moment of reckoning with my own wanderlust? Perhaps only now does it feel that way. At the time, it seemed innocent.

It seemed innocent when Carmen, at her house, said the wine was in the basement. Would I help her pick a bottle? I knew, even then, that it was a covert invitation. I accepted. I told myself again it was innocent. It's cliché to say "the next thing I knew," but the next thing I knew, we had not even looked at the wine rack. We had kissed and then dropped to the cold concrete floor, hands beneath each other's clothes. We had looked into each other's somewhat startled eyes and giggled at our own indiscretion—what I see now as our disrespect, Pete waiting upstairs, surely wondering what was taking so long. I reveled in the danger and in giving myself permission to act on my attraction to someone else, to let someone else be attracted to me. I suppressed, in the moment, the guilt that built heavy beneath my laughter.

I wonder whether I already knew, but hadn't acknowledged, that Pete's departure was already well underway, a departure far greater than the steps Carmen and I had descended to her basement. Admitting this transgression requires, now, acknowledging my own culpability, that I am to blame as much as Pete for the degrading of our relationship. It also begs a larger admission I couldn't make at the time, not then and not for years afterward. I had experimented with women years earlier, before meeting Pete, but had never considered the option of coming out, never thought that my attraction to women was anything but innocent and fleeting.

Perhaps that's why I never told Pete what happened in the basement. I also didn't tell him that, a few weeks later, Carmen walked partway home with me after my evening class on a night when Pete was playing a gig with his jazz trio. When it came time for our paths to branch, she pulled me in and tried to kiss me. "I can't," I'd said. "I'm married to Pete." There was the guilt, risen up instead of the laughter. There was the moment that could not evolve into anything like the wanderlust I felt and the wanderlust Pete had already indulged, though I couldn't have known it.

* * *

I never confessed any of this to Pete, not even after he had moved back to Chicago, not even after he had said *everything* to me, not even after I'd dropped off the divorce papers at the courthouse downtown. We were assigned a hearing date: September 15, 2011. Pete would have to return for it. I was still not over him, still in denial of his affair and our split. In all my excitement at seeing him, I returned to my old ways and began planning the gifts I would make for him. In fact, I would finally pay back to him the gift he had given me during our whole time in Missouri: meals. In the days before his arrival, I worked for hours in the kitchen, making my few signature recipes: foods I thought he might miss when he was back in Chicago. I baked chicken pot pies from scratch and froze them in individual portions. I rolled and cut homemade egg noodles, cooking them into a chicken noodle soup. I baked small ramekins of macaroni and cheese. These were the meals we'd eaten together, in Chicago, before Missouri, and I would send him home with them. When we might never see each other again, he would have food to remind him of me.

After we'd gone to court and made our divorce official, Pete came back to the house, now mine, alone, to retrieve a few things he'd left behind. One of these was a large purple cooler, a hand-me-down from his parents that we'd taken on many a camping trip. I had filled the cooler with ice, and with all the frozen portions I'd prepared.

"For when you get hungry," I said, and handed the cooler over to him.

He said thank you, but there were no tears in his eyes as he left.

A month later, winter began without him and the white house grew cold and bright. I had given up on pulling the vines from the wood siding and hired a neighbor to mow the lawn. The garden was again overgrown with weeds, so sturdy even the first frost hadn't wilted them. From the silent warmth of my office, I sent Pete an email. The subject line was "On a cold day, every sound feels louder." What I meant to say was how silent the house felt without Pete's bass scales, without the underlying beat of the metronome. My message to him read: "Some days go by that I do not think of you. Today is not one of them." What I meant to say was that I hope what is lost can never be entirely gone.

MY HANDS, REMEMBERING

Corvallis, Oregon, 2007

During my master's program in Oregon, when Pete had stayed behind in Chicago, I took a weekend trip to Bend, where I wandered into a yarn shop. Its framework bore signs that it had once been a barn, though the wood walls and rafters had been whitewashed, and the concrete floor, too. Light poured in through wide, high windows and rendered the room near-blinding, like the palest of Monet's winter haystacks—a white so bright it's light blue. Colorful yarns stacked on tall racks beckoned against the alabaster background. I lingered before a section of alpaca yarns in what seemed like endless shades.

Green was her favorite color, this I knew—but not any of these greens. Her green was an indescribable tone, not mint, not lime, and not sea green, but the color that robin's eggs would be if they were a shade of green and not blue. I had, though, seen her wear eggplant before, that deep purple like a mixture of blood and chocolate. So I picked up three skeins of the yarn in eggplant; better the right purple than the wrong green.

To be honest, I wasn't an accomplished knitter. Though I'd taught myself years before, I was always too timid to venture past basic knit and purl stitches, past making squares and rectangles—washcloths, scarves. I shied away from written patterns, favoring, instead, mindless projects that flew between my fingers as I listened to public-radio news. I was forever afraid of making a mistake I couldn't fix, not knowing what I do now: that most anything, in knitting, is fixable with enough stubbornness, a quality I'm not short on. But humbled by the simplicity of my scarves and washcloths, I had never attempted to make anyone a gift. I somehow suspected that whatever I made would not be good enough for its recipient—in this case, the green-loving Myra.

Myra was my professor and thesis adviser. Yet for all the time I spent with her, I longed to know her more. Something about her remained sequestered behind her quick but understated wit and tortoiseshell glasses, beneath sweaters that hung loose on her slender shoulders. I'd been thinking of Myra as I trekked around Bend, somehow sensing that the coarse high-desert vegetation and washed-out winter skies would appeal to her sensibility, to her penchant for the Gothic and uncanny. I cradled the small bag of eggplant yarn the rest of that day and evening. I handled it gently, the way I would anything of Myra's: my hardback copy of her memoir, my manuscripts with her comments and coffee stains in the margins, a copy of Proust's *Swann's Way* she had lent me, its edges softened by the oils of her fingertips.

* * *

In her first memoir, Myra writes about moving into a home with a vast garden—a garden she finds herself unequipped but quietly compelled to maintain. In my favorite scene, she has been given purple poppy seeds by a neighbor, who harbors dark secrets that mirror Myra's own. The neighbor instructs her to wrap the seeds in a wet paper towel, seal them in a plastic bag, and tuck them in the furthest corner of her china cabinet. She does as told, and three days later, lying awake at midnight, remembers her tucked-away seeds. So she rises, and by moonlight, digs her small hands (I have added that detail, for I know her hands are small, even smaller than mine) into the wet soil under cover of dark.

I relish, revel in, this nocturnal scene, picturing my diminutive mentor crouched in the dark. I feel, in her aloneness, in this moment, that I have seen something no one else has. After all, I had chosen my Oregon university for Myra's presence there. She wrote as I wanted to, in a beguiling tone and calm voice that felt as if it spoke only to me, as if it told me secrets no one else could be trusted with. But I wanted more. Myra, the dark, and poppies were only the start.

There were other secrets she didn't tell me, but which I found out from the program's more seasoned students. She had left that house with the garden, left the husband with whom she shared it, too, for another professor, a lanky, quiet man with impressive eyebrows. There was something exhilarating about knowing Myra's stories without really knowing her. It turned her past into a fairy tale, something whose secrets might always remain under lock and key, whose explanations might always dwell in fantastic, far-off realms. Even in that early proclivity toward Myra, I couldn't have possibly known how, in the approaching years, my life would come to mirror hers, especially in love: how my husband would leave me after two years of marriage to continue his affair; how I, too, would fall in love behind his back. I could know only, then, that this gift was my way of asking her to speak to me in the same hushed tones as she wrote. It calls into question for me, now, the nature of the gift: Do we give to give, or to hint at how we long to receive?

Even the pattern I'd chosen to make for Myra seemed to expose my intention, for it showed a long, diaphanous stole in eyelet lace, its fabric knit just loosely enough to let slip a view of the skin beneath it. I was undeterred by the complex charts and three pages of instructions. For the lace pattern, which from afar looked almost like leaves, was the only one appropriate for someone who gardened by night.

* * *

Myra and her husband lived in a Craftsman-style house close to campus. In its dim quarters, everything seemed to be made of mahogany and stained glass. This secretive cottage played host to parties when visiting authors came to town, or for no reason at all. At the most recent one, just after the start of fall classes, I had lingered to help clean up. I had reveled in being the last guest, drying dishes, opening cupboards to figure out where things belonged, covering leftover food and wedging it into the full refrigerator.

When the kitchen was in order, Myra walked with me through the hushed living room to the front door. We stood facing each other. She is shorter than I am, but otherwise my same slender size. She has chin-length, thick brown hair and lustrous, green-gold eyes. When she put her small hands on my hips and leaned toward me, smelling like lilacs and vodka, I put my small hands on her hips, too. For a moment, we just smiled. I wasn't sure what we were sharing, or what she meant by this gesture, but perhaps there was no sense to be made of it.

"Thank you for your help," she said. "For staying." And then she leaned in even closer and whispered, "I'm a bit drunk, I confess."

This was her secret, her gift to me, and I held it close during the dark, slow walk home, my hips remembering her hands, my hands

36

remembering her hips.

* * *

In Oregon, in winter, the rain didn't fall in thick sheets, but rather, in a persistent mist that collected in puddles and soaked through my leather boots. Most nights, I stayed inside, knitting in the warm breath of my electric heater. As I worked in the dim light, I felt a certain allegiance to Myra—my knitting akin to her gardening. Like her garden, the scarf beckoned to me in the middle of the night, so that I would crawl out of bed and thread its velveteen yarn through my fingers. Its dark dye stained my fingertips and cuticles a slight maroon, so that it appeared I'd been slicing beets, my skin soaking in their blood-juice. I couldn't help but think of the soil that must have lodged itself under Myra's fingernails as she planted those purple poppies. I liked to surmise, as I knitted by night, that maybe Myra was still awake, too, presiding over the last of her garden's blooms, that maybe we were in silent synchrony, relishing what could be done only under the cover of dark.

* * *

During those same months, when Myra's office was just down the hall from mine, she popped in one day as my friend Isabelle and I were perched on desks, feet resting in our chairs.

"Hello, my fashionistas," Myra greeted us, grinning at her own silliness, as she was prone to do. She could goof off with unprecedented gusto, had a wily humor behind those serious glasses.

We must have laughed, Isabelle and I, at being called "fashionistas," although to our credit, we did have the same style: a sort of hodgepodge Bohemian aesthetic, mixing unlikely textures and colors, wrapping ourselves in scarves and thick sweaters. So it was no wonder Myra had targeted us.

"What do you think?" she asked, sliding around the door and into full view. "I'm trying to look like Marketa Irglova in *Once*."

She was wearing black boots, a long, flowered skirt, and—dwarfing her tiny frame, absolutely enveloping her—what appeared to be a men's tweed blazer. A velour scarf framed her face and hung down over her shoulders. I'm tempted to say that she pulled it off, just because of her flippancy about the whole ensemble. But I admit, now, that what I envied was the confidence that made Myra glow, no matter what she wore. But at the time, I credited the outfit, the unorthodox mix, even if I didn't know what *Once* was.

I watched it the next weekend. It is the story of a love that cannot be. An Irish street musician and a Czech émigré connect through music and co-write the soundtrack of their falling in love, which is ultimately devastated when the émigré, Irglova—with her long skirts and slightly more tailored tweed blazers—confesses she is married. It is a love bound to its end before beginning, and as I watched it—as I watched this pair part and look back, just to see whether the other was looking back, too—I couldn't help but wonder whether something in this plot spoke to Myra the way it did to me.

* * *

In early spring, about the time the camellia tree outside my front window produced generous, magenta blossoms, I finished the scarf, casting off the final stitches and tucking in the stray ends with a darning needle. I wrapped it in carefully layered tissue paper: red atop purple, apple over plum. I folded and taped the ends and tied it with a length of real satin ribbon.

But it seemed I was incapable, by some unknown force, of giving her the scarf. I was afraid of what it would say, or of what it would ask for in return. I thought of it, tucked away on the top shelf of my closet, each time I sat in a cozy downtown gelato shop, watching from the balcony as customers came in and out of the early twilight. I waited for Myra, who was always the slightest bit late. The gelato shop was our haunt for weekly discussions of my thesis, meetings I arrived early to and awaited with restless paper-shuffling and sweaty palms, though I had no need to be nervous.

I heard the heels of her cowboy boots, quick clicks on the wood floor below, and then saw her come up the stairs. She was windblown, glasses wet and suddenly fogged by the warm indoors. She carried my damp manuscripts and an armload of books. She was radiant—but maybe it was just the rain. For it seemed, always, to rain on Thursdays at five p.m. On these Thursdays, I came to know Myra's easy laugh, the slight slouch in her posture, the way she brushed aside her bangs when they hung in her eyes. On these Thursdays, she learned that I had steady hands, that I was an amateur calligrapher, that my eyes turned a brighter blue when I was sad. She did not learn that I could knit, or that I was keeping hidden a gift. But I now see that something in my stance must have betrayed my attraction—the way I leaned faintly toward her, the way my voice softened, the way my gaze stayed upon her too long when I thought she wasn't looking. I justified my attraction by telling myself that Myra was my professor crush, a writer whose work I admired. Yet I recognized that in conversations with Pete, I seldom mentioned her—a deliberate omission. And as Myra and I left these evening sessions, exiting the gelato shop into the rainy-night dark, we lingered by the row of meters where her car was parked. She put her hands on my hips, and I put my hands on hers. She kissed me goodbye, though these kisses were quick taps, never prolonged, decidedly unromantic—to her. But on the cold walk home, I didn't feel the rain on my face, didn't consider opening my umbrella.

* * *

I graduated after that spring, and the still-wrapped scarf moved back to Chicago with me, into a closet in my new sewing room, in a new apartment with Pete, whom I would marry in less than a year. The ungiven gift seemed to carry Myra's presence into the two-bedroom apartment, with its exposed-brick walls and a peculiar diffused light that favored certain corners. For, within weeks, I began my own humble attempt at gardening in a backyard made mostly of concrete.

When I went to plant bulbs in our one small, abandoned strip of earth, I found the ground—and myself—hopelessly unprepared. The bed was filled with weeds so established that, even when I tugged at their bottoms, trying to dislodge the roots, I managed only a few stems that bled green in my palm. The thorny weeds were cause for even more concern, as I had no gardening gloves. I resorted to ski mittens and a slotted spoon from the canister of kitchen utensils and burrowed my way into the soil. I gasped and drew back each time I encountered an earthworm slinking beneath the dirt's surface. I dug up urban detritus: a beer bottle missing its bottom, the cellophane wrappers of cigarette packs. Myra hadn't explained it, I now understood the need to do this at night, hidden from the daylight's knowing gaze. But I carried on, digging holes in even rows with my serving spoon, tucking seeds in their beds.

Snow blanketed the garden a few months later when Myra visited for a writers' conference. She brought the Oregon weather with her: Chicago's below-zero temperatures suddenly rose to the balmy forties, and then came the rain—that assiduous mist. Our meetings in the vast, cavernous conference hotel were unplanned, coincidental, as if born of some secret force in the warm weather. Amid a crowd of thousands, we would pass in the hallway, too separated by the throng to stop and talk, but close enough to exchange glances. I boarded one of a dozen elevators to find she was in it. These moments distracted me during the sessions I sat through afterward. My conference notes are peppered with references to the scarf, to the secrets she might reveal if I revealed mine—the one I now am certain she already knew, but which I struggled to name. For certainly she saw the way, in those chance meetings, I withered under her gaze, the way my words failed me, the way a slight flush crept up my neck and face and the room suddenly became warmer. But no, I couldn't tell her, and I had left the scarf at home, accidentally on purpose.

After she left town, I unraveled the scarf, wound it back into three balls. But with the purple yarn like poppy seeds tucked away in the darkest corners of my closet, evidence of my failure—failure at what, exactly, I'm still unsure—I began to regret my decision. I vowed to make up for it, to stitch something, this time, so lovely I would have to give it to Myra, far too lovely to be kept or, God forbid, unraveled. I recalled that, one particularly cold Oregon day, she had shown up to teach class in a pair of green fingerless mittens. Someone complimented her on them, either for their beauty or, in this case, their practicality: In the creaky old building where we met, strange gusts snuck through the windows, whisking papers to the floor. Myra had responded that the mitts belonged to her teenage daughter. But she couldn't resist stealing them, just for a day, she said with a laugh. It felt like a secret.

I recalled that secret, the stolen mittens, as I began my search for a pattern. I perused books and websites, searching for one that was just right. At last, I found the pattern for a pair of fingerless mitts in worsted-weight yarn, with small, delicate cables circling the wrists and knuckles. These, I mused, would be perfect: not too ornate, but not entirely simple, either. While I wasn't yet an adept cable knitter, the maneuvers the pattern called for didn't seem nearly as daunting as that blood-chocolate scarf had, years before.

I bought new yarn, one-hundred percent merino wool in green—Myra's green—which the label called "lettuce." It was a quick project, this one, especially because I carried it with me everywhere. Even a half-hour on the subway added substance as I knit around and around on three small needles, joined to form a circular shape. I took delight in the rows that required cable knitting, not the least for how easy it seemed, now, what would once have been a struggle. In just a couple of weeks, the mittens were done. I tied off the ends and slipped them on my own small hands. They fit perfectly. Almost too perfectly; I would have kept them had I not gotten an email from Myra the next day: She was coming to town in just a few days for the Chicago Humanities Festival.

So the day before Myra's arrival, I wrapped this second gift even more carefully than I had the first. I began with a layer of blue tissue paper, in which I enveloped the gloves and taped off the ends. Over that, a small strip of Japanese-print paper wrapped once around the outside. And atop that strip of delicate, green paper pocked with cherry blossoms, a green ribbon as close to the color "Lettuce" as I could find, tied in a bow. I tucked it in my purse before I could change my mind.

We were to meet at Daley Plaza, a marble-paved, buildingless downtown block, its centerpiece a looming red sculpture by Alexander Calder. Waiting restlessly at the sculpture's base, I saw Myra and the professor crossing the broad plaza. By the time Myra reached me, she had removed her black wool coat and flung it over one arm, the day surprisingly warm. It was hardly the time, I thought, to give someone mittens. Nonetheless, after the hugs, after she had appraised me, hands on my hips—a feeling I still wilted beneath—and pronounced me "just as beautiful as always," I felt my stomach turn at the approach of my imminent task. I opened my purse.

"I made you something," I said, thrusting the gift into the hand that wasn't holding her coat.

"What for?" she asked, but gave me a knowing sideways glance.

"Open it," I said.

She sized up its wrapping, turning the small package over in her small hands. I looked down at my own.

"I can't open this," she said. I sank. "Only you could wrap a gift so that it's utterly unopenable. You should get a doctorate in gift wrapping."

But slowly, she untied the ribbon and slid off the Japanese paper without ripping it. She untaped one end of the tissue paper, leaving the rest intact, and slid out the green mittens. She handed the wrapping to the professor. "Save this," she said. And then she put on the mittens. They fit perfectly. She hugged me, something in her frame's bony defense giving way, to let me sink in, to let her be sunken into.

"The shade of green—it's perfect," she said, as we stepped back from each other. "You know me far too well."

* * *

For years, I reserved that eggplant-colored yarn for Myra. But I could never find the right pattern for it—or, that was my excuse, my reason to prolong the longing that yarn evoked. The three small balls had migrated toward the bottom of my basket as other projects took priority. The yarn's dormancy was something I became accustomed to, came to like, even. For as long as I hadn't made the scarf, as long as I hadn't given it to her, there was still room for anticipation, for possibility, for fulfillment—although I now recognize how the ache of longing constitutes its own fulfillment. With that yarn always there, stored deep down, I couldn't help but think of Myra, her purple poppy seeds buried, her thrill more in the waiting than in the blooms she never describes, but which must have sprung up, eventually.

Shortly after Myra's visit, after I gave her the mittens, I was accepted to a PhD program. Pete and I moved into our small, white house in our small Missouri town, where the low notes of his upright bass colored our own home secretive and somber, like Myra's Oregon bungalow. August is too late to begin a garden, some books said, but others were optimistic, claiming vegetables that germinate quickly and resist frost can produce well into winter's first months. Zucchini are good, these books said, and peas and green beans. So I pulled up the weeds in our front flowerbeds—the only vegetation there, to date. Planting, it was advised, should be done in the evening, since the scorching August midday could damage and dehydrate the seeds. So at sundown, I sowed even rows in the dirt, then covered the seeds with moist topsoil. Within weeks, the white blossoms of green bean plants rose tall at night, drinking of the air's humidity. Nasturtiums appeared in haphazard clusters, and beside them, a small bunch of flowers I couldn't name, but which were purple, slightly lustrous, with the saturated shade of plums past ripe—the color I imagine purple poppies must be when they emerge from their buds by night.

CEDAR LEAVES

Columbia, Missouri and Corvallis, Oregon, 2011

By September, after Pete and I had spent a mere month in Missouri, I had killed our garden with remarkable efficiency. Around that time, Myra told me that her new book was due out soon—"sort of a weird thing: partly a garden journal, too," she called it in an e-mail. This news prompted me to forget my failed garden and dig out the eggplant yarn to search for a new pattern. I wanted something with a garden theme, something subtly leafy, perhaps; that was all I knew. And I found it: a crescent-shaped "shawlette," a hybrid of a scarf and a shawl, whose edge was framed with intricate lace leaves—cedar leaves, the pattern said they were.

I began the scarf as the trees started to turn, curtaining the neighborhood in saturated yellows and burgundies. I worked with the windows open, letting in a wind turned colder each day, and heard the leaves rustle with a new insistence. With that susurrus outside came revived impetus to finish the scarf: Myra emailed, urging me to come to Washington, D.C., in February for an annual writers' conference. If beginning the scarf again did not rekindle my longing, this invitation did. It had been a year since I'd last seen her. My urgency had faded over time, though I still allowed myself to pine over emails signed with "Much love," allowed myself to misread exclamations of being "sorely missed," allowed myself to linger too long over each letter, until I had memorized Myra's delicate words, which I cherished as if they were her. So beginning in October, I planned this trip, trying to hide from Pete my excitement at seeing Myra, but basking in hopeful anticipation as I checked off another plan laid: flight, bed-and-breakfast, an alumni dinner on the night I was to arrive. All of this for the scarf, the eggplant scarf now nearly five years in the making.

* * *

February came slowly. I finished Myra's scarf two days before I was supposed to leave for the conference. Anything lace—such as those cedar leaves—needs to be set in place with a process called "blocking," which opens up the stitches and sets their shape. I soaked the shawl in water just long enough to saturate its fragile fabric, then spread out two garbage bags, edge to edge, on my office floor. Then, with painstaking care, I laid down the shawl and shaped it into a crescent, a quarter-moon. Around the periphery, I secured each leaf's edges with three metal pins. These leaves, which had been curled upon themselves, unfurled in the pinning, and in this sudden transformation I found more satisfaction than I ever had in the first leaves of any real garden.

Just about that time, as I was crouched on the floor with my pins, Pete turned on the radio. We'd heard rumors of snow, but now it seemed more serious: A bona fide blizzard, they were calling it, would blow in the next day, bringing two feet of snow to this town that would become crippled by winter weather. We listened in disbelief. I phoned the airline and moved my flight up a day. As it turned out, that one day would make no difference. Central Missouri's small regional airport would shut down for a week, its three departing flights a day reduced to zero. As snow piled up, obstructing roads and turning the city white-silent, I knew I was stuck.

For three days, snow blew against our small house, accumulating in drifts that held shut the front and back doors. It turned the world a granulated white, cast different hues by the rise and fall of daylight. And right then, I was glad I had stayed, glad to see the way the sun hung on the walls at the golden hour, the way it consumed everything for such a short time. Then white darkened to lavender, like moth wings, then to the hue of purple poppies and finally, to what we can no longer see, but what we believe, on faith alone, is still there.

Holed up, safe from the cold and accompanied by the hum of the gas furnace, with Myra's scarf still pinned to the floor next to me, I sat down at my sewing machine. I wanted to make the wrapping for this gift even better than the Japanese paper I had used on the green mitts. Paper wouldn't do; only cloth would. I cut out two squares of flower-print calico fabric and two lengths of linen ribbon, and from these, fashioned a drawstring bag. I unpinned the scarf from the floor, and the leaves held their shape, unfurled for good. I folded the scarf and slipped it into the bag. It should have been a moment of fulfillment, the completion of this scarf so many years in the making, the embodiment of a love so many years in the imagining. Instead, it seemed like I had lost something. As long as there was green merino—the green that robin's eggs would be, if they were green and not blue—and purple alpaca—like plums past ripe—running through my fingers, there was anticipation for what it could become, and for what would become in the giving of it. This felt like an end, an admission to myself that there was nothing, anymore, to yearn for.

Nonetheless, I mailed the package. I waited—two days, three. I pictured the box on Myra's porch, pictured her picking it up, puzzled, and carrying it into that secretive mahogany and stained-glass bungalow. There, perhaps on the bench of the entryway grand piano, or on the dark, imposing dining table, or maybe on the kitchen counter, beside a bottle of red wine, she would remove the tape, open the calico pouch, and run her fingers over the delicate cedar leaves. She would wrap the soft shawlette around her small shoulders, the room suddenly warmer, her face faintly flushed. I imagined this scene, over and over, when I read and re-read the note she sent me a few days later:

Lauren,

Yesterday I got your mysterious package, and late late last night I opened it, and was completely blown away by the beautiful, delicate, beyond right for me scarf. Scarf seems the wrong word here . . . it is far too ethereal for such a dowdy word. It reminds me of the lace pieces worn by Jane Austen's characters, but with such depth and variation of color. It is both comforting and magical, and that, for me, is the ultimate combination. You seem to know this, you magical creature! Anyway, upon my soul I am thrilled, and thank you. Much love, and I hope it is not too long before we see each other.

* * *

It wouldn't be long. In late May—three months after I sent Myra the scarf and just two weeks after Pete told me he was leaving me—I went back to visit my small Oregon town. The trip's timing was merely a coincidence. I'd booked it months before.

Myra and I went to brunch at a home-style spot she'd picked, a short drive into the rolling hills outside town. We sat on a heated porch covered by a green plastic roof that rang from the hard rain outside. She wore her shawlette draped loosely over her shoulders, and the eggplant yarn was lustrous against her face, in the way that all colors are exaggerated against gray, storm-torn skies.

I picked at my bacon and eggs, stumbled over my slow words. I didn't understand, I said, how Pete could be so set on leaving without giving this a second thought. How could he declare something broken without trying, first, to fix it?

Myra looked at me knowingly. She had, after all, been in the same situation.

"I'm going to tell you what you don't want to hear," she said. "He's too far gone."

She said she had been in the same position when she left her first husband: She wasn't willing to work it out, wasn't willing to look back. In her words I saw that I had doubted Pete's sincerity, had thought I could somehow bring him back to me. But no matter how many times I'd heard the truth, it only seemed true coming from Myra.

After breakfast, we ran to her car in the pouring rain, giggling at how quickly our hair became drenched and dripped on our slender shoulders. As Myra drove me back toward town on winding, country roads, the rain slowed, then stopped, and the clouds parted. Sun fell down on the green-glowing fields around us and shone brightly on the still-slick roads.

When we pulled up in front of the friend's house where I was staying, I reached down for my handbag, remembering that I had brought my copy of Myra's new book. I pulled it out shyly, reluctantly. It felt like I was asking for a favor.

"Will you sign this?" I asked, placing the book in her hands.

"Of course," she answered.

I handed her a pen I'd brought for this purpose, and in the close, still quiet of her sedan, she leaned over the book and began to write on its title page. I sat silently, trying not to look at what she was writing, as if it should only be read when I was alone, in private. There is something awkward about sitting next to someone you know is writing to you.

I thought of a night, so many summers ago, when I had run into Pete at a Chicago bar just days after one of our many breakups, after he had tearfully moved out of the first apartment we'd shared. I thought of how, as he sat next to me reading, I had pulled a blank card from my purse and began to write: "To the stranger sitting next to me who knows me so well . . ."

Myra signed her name with a flourish, closed the book gently, and handed it back to me. We both got out of her car. We stood on the sidewalk, facing each other. I put my hands on her hips, then leaned in and hugged her tightly. We pulled away from each other, waited a beat, and then hugged again. Even in this surge of sadness, this goodbye, I wanted to relish the moment, to draw it out longer. For I know, now, that to feel anything strongly, even if it is grief, is better than to feel nothing at all. To say goodbye—to our lovers, to our mentors—means that we have been blessed with the sheer pleasure of knowing them.

When she had driven away, I pulled the book from my bag and opened it. I ran my finger over Myra's words, her quick, slanted cursive: "For Lauren, with much love, enormous admiration, and high hopes."

* * *

In her first memoir, Myra writes of a restaurant she swears exists—at a bend in a road near some railroad tracks—but which she can't seem to find again. In this restaurant, the vinyl booths were a peculiar shade of green, her green. The restaurant, Myra writes, reminds her of cities we know we won't return to—cities that would save us, if only we could go back. And so perhaps, then, only Myra herself can give me the words for what remains. For I love her not the way of cities I've seen and will never go back to, but the way of cities I will never see, but long for, nonetheless.

LATE MAY, OREGON

Corvallis, Oregon, 2011

In memoriam: Isabelle Brock

December 4, 1981 – August 9, 2018

I will arise and go now, and go to Innisfree . . .

—W. B. Yeats

It was a fortunate accident, on my late-May trip to Oregon, that I ended up staying with my friend Isabelle and her six-year-old daughter, Eliza. Another friend had bailed on me, and I knew that Isabelle was still in town, teaching at the university. I confess, I was afraid to ask for her help: I'd always found her slightly intimidating—her witty but poignant writing, her self-assured sarcasm, her haphazard sense of style, her white-blonde hair and wide blue eyes. Besides, I hadn't been in touch since we'd graduated, and it felt like an imposition, calling out of the blue and asking her to put me up for five days.

But when I explained my predicament, she simply said, "Of course you can stay." I was surprised at her lack of hesitation, though I now know I shouldn't have been. This was just the first of many generosities she would offer over the week that followed. But at the time, I was simply relieved that my travel plans had been salvaged, reminded of the ways Oregon always had of redeeming itself.

* * *

Isabelle and I had gestured toward friendship in our two years as graduate students, but the gestures never quite took hold, never coalesced into the bond I'd had with others in the program. I mostly blame the fact that I was so intimidated by her, the fact that I wondered why someone like her—so talented, so beautiful—would want to become more than my mere acquaintance. But now, I see that Isabelle was the one trying and I was just too slow to catch on.

One Thanksgiving, during our two-year program, I had decided to stay in Oregon for the break. I spent the holiday in the dim quiet of my apartment, sewing, lulled out of my loneliness by the machine's gentle hum—like *hallelujah, hallelujah.*

It was mid-afternoon, the sky already lavender-gray, and I was making applique bibs with Chicago Bears and Cubs logos for Pete's nephews. Isabelle called. Somehow, she'd sensed that I had stayed, and knew I was alone for the holiday.

"I'm bringing you a plate," she said. "We had turducken. There's tons left over."

Five minutes later, she was at my front door with a foil-wrapped offering. I invited Isabelle inside, then took the still-warm food from her and set it on my kitchen counter. We chatted briefly, and I showed her my newly sewn bibs, which she held carefully, running her fingers over the zigzagged stitches. She could stay only a few minutes, needing to get back to her houseguests. But as we gave each other a quick goodbye hug, I was touched by this gesture of friendship, of caretaking.

I unwrapped the foil from the plate and noted with a smile that it was a plastic child's plate, painted in bright-colored flowers. Isabelle had piled it high with turkey and duck and chicken, stuffing, mashed potatoes, and green beans. The smell of Thanksgiving filled my small kitchen, and suddenly I longed for the warm aromas of my grandma's house, where my family was eating without me. I moved my sewing aside and sat down at my small table, digging quickly into this feast for one. The meat was tender and juicy, the stuffing dense and richly textured. The mashed potatoes and green beans, both, had just the right touch of garlic. As the sun went down and my apartment darkened, I was full and happy, switching on my lamp to continue sewing into the night. But inspired by Isabelle's generosity, a new pattern came to mind. I began sketching ideas for a small tote bag, something Isabelle's daughter, Eliza, could use to carry her artwork home from preschool or picture books from the library.

I searched through my piles of fabric and found a mint-colored calico flecked with small flowers—that would be the bag's outside. For the lining, I would use fabric from a thrift-store bedsheet, printed with orange and yellow butterflies. And on the outside of the bag, I'd cut out just one butterfly and affix it with careful applique, stitching around the edges in a thick zigzag. I was almost afraid to start sewing, afraid that the bag wouldn't live up to my expectations. But, days later, it did. And three and a half years later, in Oregon, in late May, I would see the bag hanging on a wooden hook by Isabelle's front door, ready for the library excursion that she, Eliza, and I would make together.

* * *

On my first day back in Oregon, I waited on the university campus while Isabelle taught her classes. I sat in the student union and gazed through plate-glass windows toward the Art Department building where, in a dim-lit, dusty basement, Pete and I had letterpressed the invitations for our wedding. All spring in the second year of my master's degree, I awoke early on Saturday mornings and spent hours in the underground workshop, setting type and printing test runs. Then, on a weekend visit, Pete accompanied me. My test prints were done, and it felt as if I had saved making the real invitations for just this moment. I loaded each blank card—a deep yellow color the manufacturer called "curry"—onto the desktop platen press, pulled the lever to make a black-ink imprint. Pete hung them to dry, clipping each one with a clothespin to the strings that dangled from exposed ceiling pipes. When we ran out of space for our two hundred invitations, he spread them across every open surface, so that when we were done, the worktables and typeface cabinets glowed golden. We left them overnight, and the next day, when he had left, I went alone and collected them, stacking them neatly in my hands, remembering how we'd made them together. And still, three years later, my hands remembered the cool, smooth metal of the platen-press handle, the rough dampness of the turpentine-soaked rags I used to clean black ink from beneath my fingernails.

* * *

Waiting for Isabelle on campus, I began to remember her stories, the ones she'd shared while we sat in our offices, gossiping, or when we ran into each other downtown. Once, she and her husband had gotten in a fight, she said, and he had thrown his wedding ring out their second-floor bedroom window. Later, he went down and searched

55

the street to retrieve it, his gesture of reconciliation. I thought, then, about how Pete would not wear his wedding ring when he was mad at me. He would leave for work before me, and leave the ring for me to see on his nightstand when I woke up. His gesture of reconciliation was to put it back on—until, I suspect, the day he set up his new apartment in Chicago. Until the day he went to work without the ring one day, and then left it on his nightstand for good.

In the second year of our program, Isabelle and her husband divorced. I never asked her about it, afraid to unearth the hurt that she hid with such grace. But occasionally, in quiet moments when I sat in her office after class, Isabelle told her stories the way I have come to tell my own about my divorce from Pete: straightforwardly, just the facts, trying not to let emotions creep in. But in both our stories, it is the silent spots that matter, the places where we pause, where something rises up in us that we are afraid to share, lest we actually let ourselves feel it. The deep guarding that happens in this telling wouldn't have been obvious to me when I knew Isabelle, before. But now that I have endured what she has, I can, in retrospect, see what lay beneath her stories, what she left unsaid. I mistook for distance what was, in fact, the act of saving oneself.

* * *

Isabelle and I met up in early evening, at a reading Myra was giving in the warm, bright university library. Isabelle looked the same as when I had last seen her, save for the fact that her naturally white-blonde hair was longer, now, almost to her waist. But she had the same layered style that was both her hallmark and mine in graduate school: a wool skirt with leggings and leather boots, a sweater beneath a down vest, her neck and shoulders wrapped in a thick scarf. It was May, but the Oregon nights could still be cold, bringing those last traces of winter rain and damp pavement. As we removed our layers, Isabelle introduced me to her boyfriend, John, a tall, lanky man with a thick, dark beard and blue eyes so bright it seemed as if he were always smiling. As we sat down a few rows from the podium, old friends and professors approached, and I felt like I was a part of something, again. All I had felt, recently, was my separation from Pete, but the welcome back to this town reminded me that there was a place I still belonged, even if it was halfway across the country.

* * *

After the reading, Isabelle, John, and I walked together to the after-party, held at a bar in the small downtown, just a few blocks' walk from campus. The bar was one I'd been to before, both cozy and sleek—cozy for the dim strings of Christmas lights just barely illuminating it; sleek for its concrete floors and exposed ductwork. The place was packed, voices echoing off its sparse surfaces. Looking around, I knew hardly anyone—a few old friends still in town, professors up late enough for a party. But mostly, the crowd was made up of Myra's current students, who sat together at a long table, laughing loudly and tapping their pint glasses in toasts. I looked longingly at these students, wondering whether they realized what good fortune they had, right then, to be where they were. I wanted it again. But when can we ever know, in the present, just how lucky we are?

At Isabelle's house, she set me up on the couch with ample blankets and a pillow. Her small, one-bedroom house had the delightful signs of kid habitation: a sticker collection on one wall, markers of age and height plotted on a doorframe, a bookshelf in the living room full of crayons and construction paper, games, puzzles, a fairy-princess costume. Eliza was asleep in the bedroom, having been watched by her dad while we were at the reading and party. Isabelle's bed, in a show of motherly sacrifice, was in the living room, across from the couch, behind a makeshift wall of dressers and bookshelves. Her walls were painted in bright but tasteful colors, hues of orange and blue and green that glowed softly in the lamplight. Plants—sturdy and broad, the kind only Oregon can sustain—adorned every surface in large, lacquered ceramic pots. It was a haven—for Eliza, for me—that only Isabelle could create, and I reveled in its coziness as we got ready for bed.

We talked in hushed tones so as not to wake Eliza, though Isabelle assured me she was a sound sleeper. I told her about Pete, about the divorce, and not once did it feel awkward to open up to this friend I was just getting to know. For she had opened up her house to me, had tried to open up her life and I had never returned the offer. She sat on her bed and I on the couch across from her, both of us cross-legged, knees pulled close to us. As we sipped the last of our beers, she asked, "Do you think you'll ever get married again?"

At that point, I couldn't fathom it. I could see only that I still was, technically, married. I could see only the hope that Pete and I might, impossibly, somehow, be mended. But I now know that Isabelle could see an inevitability in my situation that I couldn't. She had seen her own marriage through to its end and had moved on to love again— John with eyes so bright he seemed always to be smiling.

"I don't know," I said. "I think I could love someone again."

We lay down, covered ourselves up. Isabelle turned out the lights.

"Goodnight," we said at the same time.

* * *

I woke up to Eliza gently poking my shoulder.

"Lauren," she whispered. "Lauren! Do you want to play with me?"

"Of course," I answered, sitting up and stretching. Isabelle's daughter has always been irresistible, even at six in the morning. Besides, the sun was streaming in the living room windows, overheating the blankets I slept beneath. I remember Eliza in diapers, propped on Isabelle's hip as she stopped by the office. I remember seeing her tucked, asleep, into her toddler bed one night at Isabelle's apartment. I remember when, headstrong at age three, she had decided she no longer wanted her nickname, "Ella" (short for "Elizabeth"), but instead wanted to be called "Eliza." Isabelle had complied, alerting preschool teachers and friends, and sure enough, "Eliza" stuck. Now, she was a kid and not a toddler, but lovelier for it—her mother's white-blonde hair, her tiny, curving nose. Wide blue eyes and the declarative manner of a first-grader.

We sat on the floor and put together puzzles while Isabelle ran a quick errand—coffee for herself, a smoothie for Eliza. As kids do, Eliza quickly tired of the puzzle and wanted, instead, to draw. I saw in her so much of myself as a kid—attracted to art supplies over everything else, a love for stickers. But while I had saved my stickers as a kid—keeping them on their wax-paper backing, afraid of using them for fear I might ruin them or put them in the wrong place—Eliza used hers with abandon. She placed them carefully on blank paper and, with markers, drew backdrops. Elephants in a zoo. Tigers in a jungle. Horses in a pasture, with Crayola-yellow hay. She pressed down hard with her markers in a way I never had, not afraid, as I'd been, to use them up. I relished watching her work so confidently, unafraid of making a mistake and wasting one of those stickers I would have considered so precious.

Still, as an adult, I have the instinct to keep nice things pristine, rather than using them. I hesitate to wear my best clothes for fear of staining them, to eat off my glass plates for fear of dropping them, and to write with nice pens for fear of exhausting their ink. Eliza, like her mother did, appreciates things by using them, not by saving them. When she offered to paint my fingernails, she worked the same way: brushing on thick globs of gold-glitter polish, so that it didn't dry completely for hours. When she saw me knitting, later that day, Eliza sat contently beside me, watching my fingers work the rows of stitches.

"Can you make a collar for Cedar?" she asked. Cedar was their cat, an affectionate orange tabby who alternately curled up in our laps and asked, at the door, to be let outside, where he nibbled at Isabelle's plants, then gagged up half-chewed leaves.

"Of course," I answered.

* * *

Over the next few days, Isabelle, Eliza, and John enveloped me in their lives. They took care of me. We went for drinks at the bar that had been our favorite during graduate school, one that served up massive slices of pizza with sourdough crust, that made its own kiwi-infused gin, which I drank mixed with tonic water. Isabelle, Eliza, and I made a trip to the public library so that I could show Eliza some of my favorite children's books: the illustrations of Chris van Allsburg, the hilarity of a cartoon family called "The Stupids." Isabelle and John took me disc golfing—a new feat for me—where on my first throw I lost Isabelle's disc in a nearby blackberry bramble. Though John braved the thorns, his hiking boots best suited for the task, he couldn't find it. For the rest of the course, I walked along, occasionally taking shorter throws when there were no bushes in sight.

Isabelle and I had the same taste in music—jam bands and folksy, acoustic ballads—and we spent many a night in her cozy cottage, she playing for me new music that I quickly fell in love with. My favorite was a Susan Tedeschi cover of Bob Dylan's "Don't Think Twice": *Oh, you're the reason I'm travelin' on. Don't think twice, it's alright.* But the song Isabelle played most was by the band Elephant Revival, a song called "Feathers Rise": It's slow and melodic and begins with these words: *My lover lays me down inside the garden soil. We rest our heads upon the breast of worlds unknown. We stare into the skies and watch them come alive. We stare into our eyes, never turn our heads.* They are telling, these lyrics, of the stages of moving on. We can dwell on what's gone, or we can look toward what's new, and as I sat on Isabelle's couch, something in me turned toward looking forward, toward seeing that only without Pete would I open myself up to new moments like these.

The best day was a sunny one. Eliza had gone to stay with her dad, who lived in the same town. Isabelle's small cottage, painted purple on the outside, was surrounded by a vast garden. Early in the morning, she went outside to cut flowers: irises, calla lilies, daisies, columbines. She arranged them in vases around the house, atop the microwave and the refrigerator, places I would never have thought to beautify. She made me feel guilty about my own Missouri gardening: the beds I'd planted at the first hint of warm weather, but neglected and let die already; the aloe and snake plants I'd set on the back porch when we'd moved in and forgotten to bring inside for winter, so that they, too, died, their ceramic pots chipped and cracked by the cold.

There was an extra garden bed outside, in Isabelle's front lawn, that she had never used. It was covered with a tarp and filled with weeds. Today, she figured, she would plant it. She had some tomatoes still in their plastic nursery containers and some poppy seedlings from her ex-husband. So with Isabelle and her friend Samantha, I ventured out into the garden. I watched with admiration as Isabelle tore the tarp off the bed, unafraid of what might be lurking beneath it. She took a shovel to the moist dirt, using all her weight to wedge wilted, dead foliage from the ground. She didn't flinch at worms the way I did, just picked them up and flung them out of the way. She didn't wear gardening gloves, so that her hands became black with dirt. She turned up the soil, shovelful by shovelful, then patted it back down. While I sat on nearby paving stones, she knelt and planted the poppy seedlings in neat rows, then dug holes and situated her tomatoes.

As I went in get us some water, I noticed, hanging on Isabelle's refrigerator, a picture of her. She is naked in a claw-foot bathtub, holding an infant Eliza to her chest. Eliza is so new that her knees still curl up into her armpits, her feet bent froglike up to her shins. She rests her head on Isabelle's collarbone, on a pillow of long, wet, blonde hair. Someone—perhaps Eliza, spotting a perfectly good place for a sticker—has covered Isabelle's exposed breast with a decal shaped like a flower. This made me laugh, in spite of the inadequacies the photo evoked in me. Would I ever be able, I wondered, to take care of anything well enough that it would stay? That it would not die or crack or just slip quickly away? With glasses of water for both Isabelle and me, I walked back out into her front yard, saw her watering the planted bed. The tomatoes, already, seemed to stand taller in their new homes. The poppy starts were greener, packed so closely together. I pictured what they would become under Isabelle's hand: a broad swath of red in the bed, red and their small black eyes, their long stems, taller, still, tilting toward the Oregon summer sun.

On my last full day in town, I stopped at my favorite yarn shop, a quiet, sunlit nook on the edge of downtown. I wandered quietly among its racks of wool and alpaca, cashmere and silk, at last picking out two hanks of blue-green wool—a cabled winter hat for Isabelle. Then, a bright, variegated hank of merino—striped leg warmers for Liza Lou, as I'd come, by then, to call her. Finally, a small skein of yellow cotton—a collar for Cedar.

THE CHIPP INN

Corvallis, Oregon, 2006

In the first year of my master's program, I stayed in Oregon for Thanksgiving, though I imagined constantly how the day would have looked different, had I returned to Chicago. In late October, Pete had come to visit. We drove to the Oregon coast. We built a bonfire on the beach, listened to the Pacific waves crash against the rocky shoreline. We bought pumpkins to carve. We argued in our hotel room on our last night together, Pete folding a room-service menu in half and telling me, "This is how weak you are." When I dropped him off at the Portland airport the next day, our uncarved pumpkins remained in the trunk of my car.

A month later, in my quiet apartment, I glanced at the stove clock. It was 8:30 p.m. in Oregon, 10:30 there. In Chicago, I'd have been walking to the Chipp Inn. I'd pull my red scarf tighter around my neck and stuff my hands in my coat pockets. An online weather report said 32 degrees in Chicago, with a chance of snow. Noting the swollen clouds overhead, I'd pick up the pace, lengthening my steps on the sidewalks that line Ashland Avenue. Past the Green Zebra restaurant and the club Sonotheque, with its brushed-steel exterior and muffled techno-hymns sneaking out the front door; past the 24-hour take-out place that serves up grilled cheese sandwiches that leak fragrant grease from their white paper wrappers. I would turn right onto Fry Street, a narrow lane lined with cars and garbage bins, single-family homes packed shoulder to shoulder. No one seems to shovel their front side-walks on Fry Street, and perhaps there would be packed snow underfoot, worn clear and icy by the stream of shoes that stepped there before me, maybe Pete's among them.

The Chipp is nestled in the ground floor of a house, and the only thing distinguishing it from its neighbors is a row of neon Pabst and Schlitz signs that shine through the windows. These lights, like beacons, cast pink and blue hues onto the snow that's packed up against the building's brick sides. The windows are steamy, showing how warm it is inside, or how cold outside—depending on your state of mind.

There aren't many people here tonight—just the regulars, but no Pete. I take a seat at the bar, next to Paul, a jazz guitarist with silver hair, a silver beard to match, and kind but icy-blue eyes. On my other side is Beth, a woman about my age, a hipster recently transplanted into this gentrifying west-side neighborhood. She has a tattoo of the number 17 on one wrist (her lucky number, she once said), and hair that falls across her face with a studied nonchalance. Joe is behind the bar; he is the owner, the bartender, the maintenance man, the father, with his broad shoulders imposing a presence that's at once intimidating and inviting. He's the kind who cooks a mean barbecue for everyone on holidays or Bears game days, showing up at 7 a.m. to grill in the bar's attached garage. But he's also the one who never quite looks you in the eye, who laughs off personal questions and asks, in a God-like voice, what you want to drink next. He stubs out a Marlboro Light in the ashtray.

"Stroh's?"

"Yep."

And he slides a bottle across the bar to me. This bar—dark, shiny oak with its polish worn away by the rubbing of elbows—has been here since it opened as a gentlemen's club in the 1920s. On the wall of a back room, there are photomontages from each decade. The first of them shows a row of men in felt hats, lined up along this bar, smoking cigars. There's also the Chipp's electrical bill from the 1940s—an absurdly small sum due. A picture of someone's new Corvair, probably one of the regulars, parked out front on Fry Street. The Chipp holds on to everything: Its nostalgia hangs like a musty incense in the air, and in the grain of these photos, and in the relics that rest atop the bar and clutter the walls. So many parables have sunk into these hardwood floors, scarred from sliding barstools, and these red walls, darkened by years of cigarette smoke. The bar counter itself is a palimpsest of carved initials—the bottom layers masked by new varnish, and then a next engraving promptly etched when Joe wasn't watching.

The place has an off-kilter bar humor about it, the humor of the down-and-out and disenfranchised. There's a photo of the 1985 Chicago Bears cheerleaders, from the miracle year the team won the Super Bowl, as if we should all remember that the Bears were once good. There's a sign above the cash register that says, "Your wife can only get *so* mad. Why not stay a little longer?" And every now and then, due to its misleading name, the Chipp Inn gets letters from large hotel chains looking to buy it. Joe reads the letters aloud and we all laugh, because we know something they don't. But it's not far from the truth: It's far easier to stay at the Chipp than to leave. Kate, nursing a Pabst at the other end of the bar, comments to Joe that she's been here since three this afternoon. Part of that, I'm sure, is Joe's doing. It's always the same: At the slightest shift that signals leaving, he slides another Stroh's across the dark brown bar and says, "This one's on me."

And then there's a holler from the back of the bar—"Food's up." Two men, Joe's friends, carry in Crockpots and heavy silver trays. They array them on the pool table in the back room, and the smell of cooked meat and barbecue sauce quickly overwhelms the lingering cigarette smoke. We regulars grab paper plates and napkins, plastic forks and knives, and we load our plates until they strain with the weight of chicken wings and potato salad, mac and cheese and green bean casserole. It's all free at the Chipp, and whoever says "you get what you pay for" is wrong. The wings fall off the bone easily, juices rising from the flesh. The potato salad is cold and crisp. As we eat, more people show up—Beth's ex-husband, who takes the stool next to hers and slips an arm around her waist. She looks at me and winks, and I figure I'll have to ask her later what's going on. She has become my bar friend; someone whom I'd never know otherwise; but here, in this haven where everything is dim and slightly blurry, she opens up easily, and I feel judgment slip away. I look toward the door each time it opens, letting in cold air and new patrons, but never Pete.

In this suspended reality, there is no work the next day, no kitchen to be cleaned at home, no lover who left me crying in a hotel parking lot in another city thousands of miles away. With each drink, all of these navigate further to the back of the mind. And maybe now, it's midnight—last call on holidays. Some might wonder why we'd all be at a bar, on Thanksgiving, instead of with family. Even I wonder this. But Joe slides me another Stroh's, and the three feet of bar it travels seem the only distance between there and where I really am.

THE SINGER

Corvallis, Oregon, 2006

December, midday, I sat on the worn carpet of my Oregon studio apartment, pinning together pieces of calico fabric specked with small flowers. Even with the curtains pulled wide open, the light in the room remained dim, diffused; the Pacific Northwest's pallid sun is no match for its winter rainclouds. I was still in pajamas, a luxury afforded by two weeks' vacation from grad school. The day's project was simple: with some scraps of calico from my stash, I set out to make a small purse for a friend's daughter.

For this humble project, I didn't need a pattern. Unlike my grandmother, who pinned and traced broad sheets of onionskin onto fabric, I like to work from a drawing in my head. It starts out slowly. I measure the fabric, mark it with blue chalk pencil. I cut each piece, leaving a fringe of zig-zagged threads around the edges. Pinning the pieces together, then, is an exact act, making sure everything lines up. I remember how my grandma laid a broad, long piece of fabric across one end of her sewing table and, pulling straight pins one by one from an old candy tin, affixed the crinkly paper pattern to the cloth. Then she cut around it, using special scissors she called "pinking shears," a name I didn't understand as a child, since they were, in fact, silver with black handles. With pins in place, I sat down at my sewing machine. It had its quirks, but it was a gift, and somehow anything—especially the imperfect—seems more valuable when it has been given to me.

As I sewed, the hum of the machine—its quick, syncopated breath—sounded like *hallelujah, hallelujah*, like the weekends that I used to spend at my grandmother's in rural Indiana. Mostly these were in late fall, when my parents would head to Bloomington with their friends to watch IU football games. I was dropped off at Grandma's along the way, in the small town of Gas City. The town is a collection of old, leaning houses and broken-down school buildings. The sign above the entrance to its headquarters reads "City of Gas City City Hall." The public library, which we passed driving into town on Main Street, identifies itself as the PVBLIC LIBRARY, and I always cringed at the Roman-style replacement of U with V. Even at age six, I knew that Gas City wasn't Rome. It was a town of about 5,000 that looked as if someone had dropped it years ago, just off Interstate 69, and forgotten to pick it up. Since then, it has made national news just once, in 1992, for forgetting where its own sesquicentennial time capsule was buried. Soon, the whole lawn in front of the Pvblic Library and City Hall was dug to pieces as the mayor and 200 residents attempted to locate the capsule—to no avail. It never has turned up.

Nestled within this town, at the corner of Fifth and A streets, a block from the Holy Family Catholic Church—where my parents were married—my grandma's house was its own time capsule. While my grandmother and granddad lingered in the kitchen—she cooking and whistling, he eating Post Toasties and deliberating over a cross-word—I roamed the house. The upstairs was the best to explore. There was the room still called "Dale and Jerry's Room," where my dad and his brother once slept in twin beds with matching plaid comforters, and where the dresser drawers and closets still held a collection of high school relics. There was a rabbit's foot on a beaded chain, a felt pennant, a deck of miniature playing cards, and a scratchy wool letter jacket from Mississinewa High. Also in the closet was a small, hand-embroidered pillow—the kind my grandma had made for each of her children, and then her grandchildren. I had my own, at home, on the top shelf of my closet. I wondered whose this was. Who had left theirs behind?

In Lisa's Room, my aunt's childhood toys still sat in a small wooden rocking chair and on a window seat covered with a blue woolen cushion. My favorite, though it now strikes me as sinister, was a doll dressed in a pink jumper and stuffed with sawdust, whose head turned from side to side via a small lever on the back of her neck. Her painted-on eyes were always out of focus. But I loved that window seat, and when afternoon struck and the sun warmed the cushion, I could pass hours sitting there, paging through old *Reader's Digest* issues, of which my grandma always seemed to have an endless supply. With the bedroom door closed, I could be lost in my books or magazines until dinnertime; I could prop up a clipboard on my bent knees and draw with the special stencils my grandma had bought especially for me, or I could pretend to dust myself with the empty perfume atomizers that had once been my aunt's.

But my favorite room by far was my grandmother's sewing room. It was tucked away at the end of the upstairs hallway, lit by two triangular windows where the roof peaked. This room, as I remember it, was always warmer than the others, maybe because the heating system in this 1904 house had come, over time, to favor certain places. This warm room always seemed to have dusty trails of light filtering through it, landing and swirling on the carpet. (And one ought not to walk barefoot in there, either, my grandma always warned. Sometimes she missed a pin or two on the floor.) In a dresser that sat under one window, each drawer was filled with sewing implements, sorted by type but not color. One was a medley of embroidery floss, each tiny skein neatly bound by a rubber band to prevent unraveling. The thread occupied another drawer, some of the spools so old they were made of wood, not plastic. Another drawer was yarn, wound into tight balls of different sizes. I was allowed to make anything I wanted to with these multicolored supplies.

My go-to project was called a "God's eye"—something I suppose I'd learned in my one year of Brownie Girl Scouts. I scoured Grandma's backyard for two twigs of equal width and length. Sometimes, feeling brave, I'd steal them from the low branches of the crabapple tree next door, keeping a careful eye out for the cranky neighbors my grandma called "the Gooneybirds." I loved how the small shoots peeled from the branch, wet and flesh-colored beneath their bark. Fresh shoots in hand, I'd return to the sewing room and pick yarn from among the drawer of mint greens and raspberry reds, yellows so rich I could taste lemon meringue on my tongue. I used to sit cross-legged on the floor of that corner room, as I aligned the twigs in the shape of a cross and wrapped the yarn around them in a diamond pattern, a loop around one stick, then the next, then the next, until the yarn reached the broken-off ends of the sticks. Grandma hung them in the windows, which rattled in the wind and were cold to the touch, and from the ornate, white-painted stairposts. And though she always thanked me for my creations, at some point, the tall, narrow house ran out of room for God's eyes.

And that's when she began to join me in the sewing room. It

must have been a year or so later; I was seven or eight when she decided I should learn to sew. My mother had taught me a basic over-under stitch on some scrap fabric, but we hadn't progressed beyond that rudimentary first lesson. To my grandmother, an accomplished seamstress and quilter, this must have seemed unacceptable. As I grew older, I realized that many of my mother's attributes—her unfinished pile of mending, her preference for eating out over cooking, her modern taste—were unacceptable to my grandmother. She was never a spiteful woman, but she did have her ideas about proper mothering.

As Grandma sat in her turquoise brocade sewing chair, I stood behind her, looking over her soft, rounded shoulder. She threaded the machine with magenta thread I had picked from the dresser drawer, then tucked a piece of scrap fabric beneath the presser foot.

"Watch, now," she urged, showing me how her foot pressed down on the electric pedal and the machine seemed to take off. The thread spool turned circles on top of the machine, the fabric seemed to move of its own accord beneath the presser foot, and a pink line of perfect stitches appeared beneath my grandma's swollen, wrinkled fingers. And the machine sang its whirring hymn—*hallelujah, hallelujah.* When Grandma let up on the foot pedal—which reminded me of the brake in my mother's big blue Oldsmobile—the machine came to a halt and quieted. Grandma tripped a lever in the back of the machine, and the fabric came free. She clipped the pink thread with a pair of nearby scissors and handed me the creation.

"That's nothing," she said. But I examined it closely, running my fingers over the even-stitched line of pink that looked nothing like the awkward, taut stitches I'd produced by hand under my mother's tutelage.

Grandma let me try, then, though my feet barely reached the

pedal. With a new piece of scrap fabric firmly secured under the presser, I gave the pedal a light tap. The machine whirred, a sort of purring that bespoke a motor almost in motion. I pushed harder—a lot harder—and we were off. The old metal Singer seemed to eat the fabric right out from under my fingers. I couldn't keep hold of it, couldn't seem to feed it straight under the needle that bobbed up and down faster than I could even see. I let up on the pedal and Grandma gave a good-hearted chuckle.

"It goes pretty fast, huh?" she asked. "You'll get used to it."

Grandma smiled at me, rubbed her liver-spotted fingers over my pale, bony knuckles. She had an easygoing demeanor but a quick, biting wit. Perhaps it's what came of raising four children and losing one. I've only heard my Uncle Dennis, born dead a year before my dad, mentioned once. He would have been her first child, and there was a lingering sense, in Grandma's house, of holding on to what we might rather forget.

Shortly after my grandfather died, in 2001, I went to visit my grandma. Since those childhood football games, I'd not been alone with her in the towering blue Victorian. It felt strangely empty compared with the holiday visits I'd grown used to, when aunts, uncles, and cousins filled the house and the smell of pie crusts wafted through the air. Now, the house was empty not only of family, but of my grandfather, as well. In his last years, my grandmother had made it her life's work to take care of him. His Parkinson's disease grew progressively worse, taking away his ability to write by hand, play games of bridge at the Holy Family Catholic Church, and finally, to feed himself, clothe himself, and walk.

My grandmother had taken care of him at home until he required the use of a wheelchair, which could not fit through the doorways of the old house. Certainly, my grandmother must have felt guilty to admit—for the first time in their marriage—that she could no longer care for her husband. For even when he lived in a nursing home, my grandmother spent every day at his bedside and every evening laundering his clothes and cooking his next day's meals. The nursing home did his laundry, of course, and provided his food, but my grandmother insisted they didn't do either of these things properly. Once, someone else's flannel shirt had been hung in my grandfather's closet by the laundry service. And the food was both bland and too salty at once. I'm sure she wondered, then, how to fill her days after my grandfather died.

On the day I visited, she showed me her sewing and knitting projects and the books she was reading. We paged together through a volume of James Whitcomb Riley's poems, which she had read to me as a child. I asked whether I could take the book home, so that I could read back through the poems I'd once known by heart. "Yes, but bring it back," she said. For certainly, her attachment to the memories the book evoked was as great as mine. But I did not return the book, I am ashamed to admit, so it sits next to me as I write. Still, there is a bookmark—the torn-off flap of a red envelope—wedged between the two pages where "Little Orphan Annie" appears:

An' the Gobble-uns'll git you
    Ef you
        Don't
            Watch
                Out!

I also realize, looking at a photo of Riley on the inside cover, why my grandma might have liked him so much: He bears an uncanny resemblance to my grandfather. They shared the same large nose, gray hair cut in a short, military style, and deep-set brown eyes. Both wore glasses, which seemed to hide their gaze even further.

With Riley tucked in my suitcase, my grandma and I went upstairs to her bedroom, where she pulled a shoebox from her closet. She carried it downstairs and I followed. We sat on the couch, and between us she laid the contents of the box. There were some of my grandfather's medals from World War II, when he had been stationed in Versailles. As she flipped through a thick pile of photographs, I realized why these were the photos she hadn't placed carefully in family albums along with the others.

"Here's Freddy with some lady in France," she said, seemingly unbothered, in the way time and death turn even our great concerns petty.

Sure enough, the black-and-white photo showed my uniformed grandfather with his arm around a woman. The couple appeared in several of the photos, and my grandma did not try to hide them from me. Instead, I think, she was letting me in on a secret that, up to that point, had been shared only by her and my grandfather, another secret the house harbored in the relics confined to its closets.

My grandparents were not yet married—they would marry after the war, on July 13, 1947—but they knew each other before Freddy, as my grandma always called him, went away. During wartime, she would do what countless other women across the country did to support the war effort: She would go to work, in her case at the Owens-Illinois Glass Factory, which made beer, soda, and milk bottles. She never spoke of this job, but I imagine the clatter of glass on conveyers all around her, the hairnet itchy on her forehead, and worst of all, the knowledge that Freddy might come home with a war bride—or might not come home at all.

* * *

In my first sewing lesson, Grandma pulled the lever on the back of the machine and extracted my crooked, wrinkled hunk of cloth. I hated that piece of cloth as much as I'd loved the act of running it through the machine. This was going to be harder than I thought, harder than Grandma made it look. For a while, I didn't want to try again. I said I just wanted to watch. This is always how I've been—afraid of trying for fear of messing something up—especially the sewing machine, although that Singer was like a tank, down to its green gunmetal shell. I wanted to watch more, from the safety of behind Grandma's shoulder. She was making a dress of mauve silk taffeta, though I couldn't have named the fabric at the time. The dress was for my younger sister, who'd be the flower girl at my Uncle Jerry's wedding. For hours, I watched as she cut and pinned, then moved over to the machine, which her age-spotted hands kept at bay far better than my small fingers could—better than they do today, even.

Nor was my own sewing machine any match for the old metal Singer. It was white, plastic, and called "Europro," a name emblazoned on the front in large, blue-painted letters that seem fleeting compared to the Singer's deep-grained engraving. But its tendencies were the same: A little push on the pedal and it made that strained, purring sound. A little harder and it was suddenly in fifth gear. And as I sewed on that Oregon afternoon, I felt as if I were still in Gas City, not so much undertaking a project myself, but instead, standing behind Grandma's shoulder in that small corner room. I looked at the back of her gray hair, styled once weekly at the local beauty salon. The stiff web of gray curls, having been slept on, was parted a bit in the back. Bending intently over the table, we moved in tandem: careful pinning, cutting, settling the fabric just right under the presser foot. She and I sewed the outside of the child's purse first. The mint-green calico stitched up easy without bunching in the machine. Changing the spool, we switched to the thread that matched the lining, with its print of monarch butterflies, tangerine orange and licorice black—poisonous, though you'd never know it from their sumptuous colors. Finally, we attached a set of satin ribbon handles. I heard Grandma pondering their durability—ribbon will fray—but running her hands along their cool grain and attaching them anyway, a quick sweep through the machine, just a few stitches, a few utterances of that quiet *hallelujah* as the afternoon exhaled a dusty, yellow light.

THIS CITY SINGS YOUR SONG

Prague, Czech Republic, 2011

What I remember most about my second trip to Prague, in July of 2007, is the heat. My first visit to the city had been in February, a year and a half earlier, so it was cold that I expected, and the oblique, dusty light of Prague in winter. We remember things as we first found them, and expect that when we return, they will not have changed.

On ninety-degree days, I reveled in the cool, concrete-smelling air of Metro stations, stories below ground level, and I took trains to museums to pass the hottest midday hours. In the evenings, as the sun slipped behind the taller buildings in the neighborhood of Holešovice, I sat and read on the brick-paved patio of the hostel where I was staying. I read innumerable books that summer, keeping cool beneath shade trees and immersing my feet in a plastic children's pool someone had placed on the patio and filled with frigid hose water. The one ritual the heat couldn't stop me from was taking the tram every day to the English-language bookstore, Shakespeare a Synové—Shakespeare and Sons. My copies of Raymond Carver's *Cathedral* and Jhumpa Lahiri's *Interpreter of Maladies* have prices penciled in Czech *koruny* on their title pages, reminders of where they were bought and read.

My other reprieve from the heat was the hostel's basement kitchen, where thick brick walls kept the room dank and damp. Sitting on a long bench at a broad, mahogany table, I penned postcards to Pete, then still my fiancé, chronicling the day's languor. Postcards had been a hallmark of both Pete's and my trips to Prague. After my first visit in 2006, he had followed suit shortly thereafter on a tour with his architecture school. In fact, our trips had overlapped so closely that I met up with him at Chicago's O'Hare Airport as I was arriving and he was departing. Both of us have endless artifacts of the other's time in Prague. Pete still has the postcards I sent, but I penned drafts of them in my journal, so I'm able to look back and see what I wrote. Mostly, it seems, I missed my old Prague, my winter Prague. I wanted to return to the places where I had missed Pete, where I had tried to conjure his presence next to me. I was nostalgic for my own nostalgia.

Things were, after all, different now between Pete and me. On my first trip, we had been broken up but not entirely, distant and hesitant after one of the many splits that characterized our relation-ship. We had been college lovers, and were on and off again for years afterward as we negotiated our careers and graduate school. But he had come around, I always said, stressing without realizing it our cycle of breakups and getting back together, a cycle I thought had finally ended.

Summer gave me a different city from the one I'd remembered, and being engaged to Pete—as if it were a license to long for him—changed my outlook on Prague and the nostalgia it evoked. On my first visit, I had liked the way I missed him when I was there, a missing exacerbated by distance and one that could continue even after I returned home, because even there, we were no longer together. This time, the missing would be left in this heat-stricken city. This time, the longing would end with my return to Chicago, to Pete. Aware of my own attraction to nostalgia—perhaps embarrassed by it—I wrote this in a postcard to Pete:

I'm writing away the afternoon—again, rainy—at Kavarna, a small restaurant near Sir Toby's [Hostel]. I was here before, in the last days of my trip. This repetition, some might say, is too easy, is at the cost of further discovery. But . . . some reminiscence is consoling. It is a mindset both new and old I fall into here, a comparison of what was and what is. Of where I'm first drawn and where I can't help but return. Nostos, Kundera would call this. It's a word Praha continues whispering in my ear, as if wanting to relive something that's at once the same and vastly different—iterations not unlike those of love itself.

One night, Pete emailed me this:

[Subject:] *The Storm . . .*

[Text:] *. . . outside is one to make love to. lightning flashing so close so often that the constant thunder allows no counting, of seconds, of distance.*

I wrote a response in my notebook, though I'm unsure whether I sent it to him:

Your words left me awestruck and unable to send anything. Thank you. So I sat in the courtyard at Sir Toby's with my notebook and morning Diet Coke, picturing your night to my first daylight, your storm to my sun. I imagined how, long after my arrival, an endless stream of letters and postcards will follow me to Chicago. How my words to you will continue to travel the distance long after it's been closed. And you will read them with me in the room and know what I was thinking on the days I've seemed silent. Time, like everything else, is malleable if we let it be.

What I longed for, it's clear from these conversations, was to repeat my first trip to Prague, to challenge Milan Kundera's notion that eternal return is impossible. In *The Unbearable Lightness of Being*, Kundera writes, "The idea of eternal return is a mysterious one, and Nietzsche has often perplexed other philosophers with it: to think that everything recurs as we once experienced it, and that the recurrence itself recurs ad infinitum!" Return, he says, is a burden, and "if eternal return is the heaviest of burdens, then our lives can stand out against it in all their splendid lightness." I did not want lightness, if lightness meant constant change—the inability of the colors cast upon Monet's haystacks to ever, again, be the same. I longed for Prague to be the same as it had been the winter before, longed to relive the two weeks I'd spent there. Again, here's Kundera: "In the sunset of dissolution, everything is illuminated by the aura of nostalgia." The way I saw it, I had spent those two weeks reveling in my independence, enjoying my aloneness, though I now see that I carried Pete everywhere with me on that trip. What I was really searching for was a memory of yearning for him—for a time when I did not have him, and longing was its own source of fulfillment. Sometimes, I think, we want simply to desire—more than we want the thing we think we desire.

Many years later, after Pete had married me and then left me one last time, for good, I would reread these lines from Margaret Atwood's story "Hair Jewellery" (from a collection purchased at Shakespeare a Synové for 350 *koruny*) and be unable to shake from my mind the Prague of that summer: "I realized I had come here not to get away from you, as I had thought, but to be with you, more completely than your actual presence would allow."

As my own postcard had predicted, Prague offered me something "at once the same and vastly different." I longed to return to Restaurace Amsterdam, the small, cozy place where I'd had my first meal in Prague, back in 2006. I looked back fondly, now, at my discomfort—a jet-lagged haze and the surprise of the introspection that comes with not understanding the language spoken around you. I had found the restaurant by accident, perhaps drawn to its bright-blue exterior. I had taken a seat—trying to look purposeful in my solitude—and in my notebook sketched a lamp hanging over the bar: an orange metal shade above an exposed bulb. All the tables and chairs had been wood of a soft, brown hue, and with rounded backs. The walls had been a light orange, the color the sunsets here were said to be, sinking into the Vltava River. In front of me, on the bar, sat a stack of books. The titles on their cloth spines were all in Czech, of course, but I had recognized Robert Penn Warren's name—the author of a title I might have known in English. *All the King's Men*, perhaps? I had turned back to my notebook, sketched a few more cross-hatchings on my lamp drawing, added a caption: "Lamp. Restaurace Amsterdam." I hadn't known the Czech word for lamp—so simple an object. It turns out I could have guessed it: *lampa*.

The waitress had placed a plate in front of me, then. What I'd ordered had been translated as "chicken steak with vegetables and lemon." My chicken steak was, in fact, a breaded chicken breast, garnished by cucumbers, red peppers, and two wedges of lemon. It smelled fried, rich, delicious. And it was. The thin-pounded, crumb-crusted meat, sprinkled with a bit of lemon, had been the best meal I'd ever eaten, perhaps because it was my first in Prague.

Determined to return, to recreate this scene despite the season and the heat, I took the Metro to the Jiřího z Poděbrad stop, across town from where I was staying. I didn't take a map, for the restaurant's precise address, or even the street name, was unimportant. Instead, I hoped my memory would kick in, would supply me with the path I'd walked so many times on my previous trip. Outside the Metro station, I headed toward the Art Deco–style Church of the Sacred Heart, whose presence had always helped me get my bearings. I knew to go right out of the station, along the main avenue, and then to take another soft right at a corner hardware store. I was relieved to see old landmarks still there, where I'd left them: the church and hardware store, an Italian restaurant where I'd eaten mediocre pizza alone one night, the hostel where I'd stayed. All of these led me to Amsterdam, still there, its bright blue exterior freshly repainted. Inside, too, it remained unchanged. I took the same seat I had before, ordered ham and cheese *krokety* and a Pilsner Urquell, and wrote this to Pete:

Restaurace Amsterdam, early afternoon. It is nice to find that the real havens have not changed. The sun from outside casts a light I'm unused to, but my favorite seat hasn't moved. There is still the empty one next to me, too, where you belong.

I wish, now, that I could have learned to enjoy my aloneness. My constant writing to Pete, attempting to share every moment with him, was what I most valued—about an experience that did not involve him, at all. Somehow, I suppose, stories become real only by our having shared them. What we entrust to memory risks being forgotten. What is written, though—what was shared on those postcards—feels substantial, enduring. But all that I captured was my longing for Pete, not the sense of independence and self-sufficiency that certainly must have overtaken me at times. Seldom did I record my own pride at navigating Prague's winding streets or ordering from a menu—my Czech still not great, but passable after months of self-teaching. These things happened, I know they did, but I must have deemed them forgettable, for they went unrecorded.

* * *

One languorous afternoon, as I sat in the hostel's brick-paved courtyard, reading and dunking my feet in the kiddie pool, I heard music from the open windows of a nearby apartment. I looked up, traced the sound to the third floor of a stucco building next door. The lyrics were in Czech, but I did not need to understand the song's words to grasp its somber mood. A woman with a lilting vibrato was accompanied by an accordion, but nothing like the traditional Czech accordion songs that buskers played in the streets near the castle and Old Town Square. Applause at the end of the song told me the album was a live recording. I also figured the music had to be local, for it bore no resemblance to the popular music played on Czech radio, which alternated between frenetic dance-club numbers and American pop ballads from the 1980s (the Scorpions' "The Wind of Change" seemed an especial—if not eternal—favorite). I became determined to find out who this singer was, and the name of the album, as if to preserve the simple memory of sitting away afternoons like this one, and as if to bask in the coincidence of this music having made its way to me—music whose words I did not know, but whose longing I did.

I paid for a few minutes of Internet time inside the hostel and began Googling phrases: "Czech accordion music." "Czech accordion woman live album." The first band that came up—whose name I wrote in my journal—was Čechomor. But further digging revealed they were not what I was looking for: a photo on the band's website showed seven middle-aged men in various states of costume, a sort of Eastern European knockoff of the Village People. I must have searched again,

84

because immediately beneath Čechomor I've written "Radůza – Vše je jedním [All is one]." I must have known, then, what I was looking for, must have set out to find it despite the mid-afternoon sun. I liked challenges of this sort in Prague—the idea of having to "set out" to do something that would have been mindlessly simple at home: to buy a CD. But I embraced such tasks with a combination of excitement and fear. Even if I could find a record store on my map, and could figure out the proper tram route to get there, could I communicate what I wanted to buy?

My map of Prague was old, but I was sentimentally attached to it. It was a map Pete and I had passed back and forth after our respective Prague trips, becoming worse for the wear with each use. It was a map I'd picked up from a "free" rack in my first hostel. After a handoff at the airport, Pete took it on his trip next, returning it dog-eared and torn at its creases, and penned with memories of me. Near the Old Town Square, "Is it right to sing Tom Waits loudly? Will these stairs answer?" And in Letná Park, north of where the Vltava River snakes through the city, Pete wrote, "I was afraid of having your trip. But instead, it is like you are here with me, guiding me through a wonderful journey of reactions and reflections." In Žižkov, near Restaurace Amsterdam: "What is it about women with braids? Lovely." (At the time, I often wore my waist-length hair braided in two ponytails that I wrapped around my head like a crown.)

Reading around Pete's words, I used our map dutifully on my second trip, though I feared it would crumble in my hands for its fragility. The more pressing problem, it turned out, was that time had rendered it hopelessly outdated. When I went searching for a record store to buy the Radůza CD, I headed toward a small row of shops near the fifteenth-century Jewish Cemetery, where the map said I would find a store called "Second Hand CD & LP." What I found instead was a row of upscale clothing and jewelry stores: Prada, Cartier, Fendi.

I'm not sure what I did then, but somehow, I found a music store. I showed the store employee my notebook, in which I'd written the name of the album, which luckily, the store had in stock. I remember most of all the swelling sense of pride I gained from moments like these, of self-sufficiency, of overcoming the fear of completing small errands in a foreign country. I did not have with me a CD player to listen to my new purchase, but during the rest of my time in Prague, I would hear Radůza as I sat in the hostel's courtyard, a reminder of what I now remember most about that trip: resourcefulness, solitude, postcards to Pete, and the light of Prague in summer.

* * *

By December of 2011, four years had passed since my return to Prague and three months since my divorce from Pete. Trying to embrace being alone, I decided to take a trip during the month-long winter break. I had several manuscripts in need of revision, and I thought that getting away from home would help. I'd be focused. I'd be inspired. I suppose that I chose Prague for its familiarity, for my ability to travel there on a budget and with minimal planning. Or maybe I wanted to return to the place where I'd longed for Pete, so that—like other times—I could feel my nostalgia for our relationship more strongly than I'd been able to in the Missouri house we'd shared for just eight months.

After our divorce, he had surrendered all the major belongings to me without a fight: furniture, kitchen tools, electronics. All these reminders of our time together made the house still ours, not mine alone. Pete had packed up his clothes, zipped his upright bass in its giant nylon case, and left. He had always traveled light, perhaps for ease of leaving. I wasn't so much sad living in the house as bored, as if always unsure what to do next. I would resist returning home after a day of classes, stopping on the way home to eat dinner at a restaurant or do homework at a coffee shop. I was figuring out how to be alone, how to occupy by myself the space of a life built for two.

I must have known that this third trip would be different, though I tried to make it resemble the previous two. I stayed at the same hostel, though this time I splurged on a private room with a double bed, a kitchenette, and its own bathroom, rather than a shared shower down the hall. When I arrived and first set foot in the room—which was on the top floor of the hostel, with its own narrow wooden staircase leading to the door—it was mid-afternoon. Though I was jet-lagged, I began unpacking, laying folded clothes in the wardrobe, arraying toiletries on a shelf in the white-tiled bathroom, arranging my knitting projects on the loveseat, and setting up my computer on the kitchen table so that, sitting before it, I'd be warmed by the sun that came in through the south-facing windows. Everything about my arrival felt half-new and half-familiar, especially the light in Prague in winter, a diffused brightness that stretches in long, elliptical beams.

My days were a mix of working on my writing and revisiting old haunts. I would get up as early as my jetlag would allow, take the couple of steps to my small kitchen counter, boil water in the electric kettle, and steep mint or chamomile tea, warming my hands over the steam. I wrote until I grew restless, and at lunchtime would walk up the street to the small grocery store, where I would buy a baguette. I brought it home and slathered it with jam and butter or made a sandwich of hard cheese and tomatoes—all of which I kept in a plastic bag that hung outside my window, secured by a knot to the inside latch, since the room lacked a refrigerator.

After lunch, I wandered, usually without consulting a map, for I was able to navigate the city innately, even after more than four years away. I found Shakespeare a Synové still in its place in the Malá Strana neighborhood, on the west bank of the Vltava, and stopped by daily for a new book, which I would read in the evening on my loveseat, watching dark, spindly trees sway outside the window. I hiked to the top of Petřín Hill in a light snow that turned to hard, driving rain, chasing me and other tourists quickly down the hill's descending paths. I was grateful, then, to find the small, dim Shadow Café—so named for its location in Petřín Hill's shadow—still right across the street, so that I could warm up with a cup of strong black tea before heading home.

According to the itinerary penned in my journal, I set out to re-find Restaurace Amsterdam on December 22, my second full day in the city and the winter solstice. This search for nostalgia is turned mundane by the items surrounding it on my list: "postcards, museum (Kampa?), buy Metro pass." I remember that it was dark by the time I exited the Metro at Jiřího z Poděbrad, night falling early on this shortest day of the year. I walked toward the Church of the Sacred Heart, where on this night there was a Christmas craft market on the broad lawn out front. When I arrived on the block where Amsterdam should have been, its neon Pilsner Urquell sign was missing—or just burned out, I'd hoped. But when I reached the building where I was sure the restaurant had been—there was the door, there, the two windows into the dining area, there, the other two windows into the bar—it had simply vanished. Lacy curtains hung in the windows, though no lights were on behind them. The building's bright-blue façade had been painted beige. In fact, the whole building was cleaner and more sterile than I'd remembered it, perhaps having received a facelift since I'd last visited. I walked up and down the block, on both sides of the street, hoping that my memory had failed me, that I simply needed to turn another corner and I'd find my old haunt. Months later, back home, I checked to confirm that I had been in the right place. An outdated website listed Restaurace Amsterdam's address as Ježkova 10. A Google street view of the address showed no restaurant, just a beige apartment building.

I turned and walked back toward the Metro. I slowed down in front of the church and wandered through the market stalls, their wares illuminated by bright lights. I bought a glass of *grog* (sugared, spiced rum) from a sidewalk vendor. I couldn't help but think of the German-themed Christkindlmarkt in Chicago, where Pete and I had gone every winter when we'd lived there. Row after row of wooden huts set up in Daley Plaza sold spiced nuts, hand-carved tree ornaments, pretzels with cheese sauce and mustard. Pete and I had wandered around, looking at the wares until our noses and fingers went numb, then sat in a heated tent that smelled of stale beer, sipping Glüwein from our souvenir mugs. My cup of grog here was made of foam, and I let it warm my hands as I walked from stall to stall, surveying hand-knit hats and felt slippers. I felt remarkably alone, invisible, walking beneath strings of tiny, twinkling lights.

I missed my nostalgia, the longing for Pete that had colored my earlier trips. This time, he was gone and not coming back. He had proved that Kundera is right, and eternal return is impossible. Even longing cannot happen the same way twice. Perhaps we are light, after all. Perhaps I am lighter alone, unburdened of my longing. Perhaps, even, I can admit to myself now, I am the kind of person who is meant to be alone, but afraid to be. If what I really want is to long, to live submerged in the fog of nostalgia, I am not sure what I gain by being with someone. Maybe it is this: that I would choose to be with someone so that I could leave them, or so that they could leave me, and then the real love would emerge in the wanting, rather than the having. What we have, we scarcely see. What we want, we see everywhere.

* * *

The story of Prague, like the story of Pete, is one of losing things and then finding them again. But it calls into the question the nature of finding, itself. Can the act be called "finding" when really, what I was doing was searching? I see, now, that finding would have been a coincidence, the kind of chance meeting that leads us to believe in fateful intervention. But go searching and you are bound to find something, even if it's not what you were looking for. And you think that because you've found something, it was what you wanted, what you needed. Perhaps this is Kundera's objection to eternal return: that our first experience can never be matched. We can replicate it, thinking we have re-created it, but we will not have. We will merely have convinced ourselves that repetition—a re-finding of the original—is possible, that change can somehow be stalled or averted.

During Pete's first trip to Prague, I received a postcard dated March 15, 2006. On the front is an abstract image of skyscrapers, rendered in black, purple, and red against a turquoise background, along with the words "Museum Kampa." On the opposite side, in tiny penciled handwriting, Pete has written "This city sings your song" over and over, filling the entire blank space. The last line, however, reads differently—simply "This city sings." And Pete was right. Even with the sentence truncated, the repetition interrupted, the city still sings. It needs to belong to no one. This city sings the song of what we lose and cannot find again, the song of what goes away and will never come back exactly the same, and what grows dark early—like the sky in Prague in winter.

90

BY BEING WRITTEN, THEY WOULD DISAPPEAR

Chicago, Illinois, 2008

This is what I know about a woman named Charlotte: More than twenty years ago, she traveled from Germany to study abroad in the United States. She spent one year at a high school in Chicago's suburbs, where Pete was a junior. After she left, the two of them kept in touch via letters, letters that increased in frequency and, I suspected, intensity as the years passed—though I couldn't be certain; Pete always kept the letters well out of my view. I cobbled together bits and pieces that he told me, held tightly to any mention of her, trying to make this person whole. Charlotte was a ballet dancer and a university student. She was a vegetarian. She had eyes that weren't brown, nor were they green—something in between. She didn't ski because making trails required that trees be cut down. She listened to classical music and mailed Pete CDs that he never listened to in my presence. I write about her in the past tense because when I lost Pete, I lost track of her, too. My perspective couples her with Pete, and now they are both gone to me.

I also knew that she was beautiful. Pete showed me a picture of her shortly after we had started dating. It was black and white, a close-up portrait, her chin resting in the palm of one tiny hand. Unpainted nails. She had a widow's peak, and straight hair that fell in soft wisps around her forehead and temples. Though she looked away from the camera, her eyes—as Pete said—were piercing. Something about the way light caught them from the side suggested her glance was always an elliptical one. But knowing all this was never enough.

There is something about a lover's previous lovers that has, from the very first, inspired a great pining in me. It was as if, because Pete longed for Charlotte, I did, too. I felt entitled to share his attraction to her. My fantasies were allowed to take full flight when Pete went to visit Charlotte in Germany, in December of 2005. We had been dating for three years—or, more accurately, alternating between breaking up and getting back together. At this point, we were broken up but still in touch. I arrived at his apartment one night and found him at the computer, booking a plane ticket.

"I'm going to Germany," he said, in the low, quiet tone of an apology.

"To see Charlotte," I supplied for him.

He nodded silently and shut the laptop, trying, I'm sure, to hide his excitement. Despite his reticence—almost shame—about it, this move was, at the time, akin to him packing a suitcase. It was so obvious as to be cliché: His ticket to Germany was the gesture of the lover leaving me. I left his apartment, and as I walked the darkened sidewalks home, resigned myself to losing him again. I'd become accustomed to his leaving, and consoled myself with the knowledge that he had always come back, that his leaving had never been for good.

He left for Germany just a month later. For the two weeks that he was there, I looked obsessively at the clock, calculating what time it was in Leipzig, what Pete and Charlotte might have been doing together. I pictured romantic dinners, glasses of wine (red, I guessed she favored) reflecting castle views at twilight. Then they were at a pub together, then walking tipsy through the quiet, snow-brushed streets, her gloved fingers entwined with his. And then there were the late-night talks in her apartment, the ones that culminated in the inevitable kiss. And though he had originally agreed to sleep on her couch, one long, lithe dancer's arm pulled him into the bedroom. I could even picture her naked. I knew she was thin, but in my fantasies, she grew even thinner, with hipbones that protruded, pulling taut the flesh of her stomach, which was almost blue in its pallor. She had a waist that curved in, the perfect contour of an hourglass. And—my god, why did I allow myself this?—small, slightly pointy breasts, again in that blue shade of pale. I saw the way her wispy hair fell over her face and bare shoulders as she slept, and the way his tender, sturdy hands brushed it away. My imagination made me a voyeur, an intruder on their interlude.

When Pete came back, I could tell his mind was still overseas, in Germany. I didn't hear from him for days. Finally, I nudged my way into his plans: a night out with friends. We were in Chicago's Wicker Park neighborhood, first at a sushi restaurant. We sat next to each other at dinner, but he didn't rest his hand on my knee in the way I'd grown to know—and which, then, became more valuable for its absence.

I talked about the teriyaki chicken I had ordered, how good

it was, even though it was mediocre and dry. About what kind of wine I should order next. About the previous two weeks, how they'd been. I tried to make them sound exciting, as if he'd missed something, as if I were worth missing. I talked about everything but Charlotte. But I could see that his thoughts, nonetheless, were still of her. His face was half-turned toward me, his eyes focused somewhere between my head and the ceiling, only rarely coming down to meet my stare, which I suspect contained more than a hint of desperation. He drank two bottles of beer, seeming not even to taste them.

When we walked to a bar afterward, trailing behind a group of other friends, I kept my hand by my side, so that he could reach for it easily as he always had. But he didn't. It's funny how those gestures become such a part of us that we scarcely feel them until they're gone, like an amputee's phantom limb. And I swear my fingertips tingled that night, almost reaching out for his hand but determined not to make a move, as if we were on our first date again.

* * *

Pete and I had been dating only a couple of weeks when I found out about Charlotte. I had spent the night with Pete in his room at the frat house, and I found myself there alone when he left for class. I decided, in the thoughtfulness that characterizes those first stages of love, to clean his room for him. I picked up bowls of hardened macaroni and cheese and washed them in the bathroom, using hand soap and paper towels. I stacked his binders and notebooks neatly on his desk chair. Under a small, wooden end table lay a ragged pile of papers. It was an accident that I found them, but no accident that I looked closely at them. In that pile, sandwiched against one another, were hand-written poems—love poems, I quickly realized, to someone he called "Lotte."

I remember only the first line of one: "My muse has gone to stroll the walks." He had never mentioned this Lotte, but already, I was jealous of her. He had a muse, and that muse wasn't me. I couldn't have known, then, that she would linger for so long, coming back to haunt a night in a Wicker Park bar, three years later.

There, I asked him: "So what was your favorite part of the trip?" It was a tradition we'd always had, one I inherited from my father, asking what the best part was. He paused. He has deep-set blue eyes that seem to disappear in the shadows of his browbones when he doesn't want to meet my gaze. Finally, he said, "The time I spent with Charlotte."

"Did you kiss her?" I blurted out, emboldened now that he had spoken her name.

"That's for me," he said. "There are things I just want to keep to myself."

And I knew he had, and that my visions had been partly true. But I wanted the details. I wanted to know how far gone he really was, with that phantom feeling of his hand still hovering above my knee.

* * *

After that trip, and Pete's quiet account of it, Charlotte appeared and disappeared in our relationship for two more years. After a long disappearance, one that saw Pete and me take a trip to Zagreb, Croatia, saw him down on one knee in the town square at twilight, she reappeared in a way that was fierce and all-consuming. We had moved into an apartment together on Chicago's west side, and perhaps the presence of her letters in my own home was just too much to resist. They called to me from some hidden place, as if Charlotte herself was a ghostly third inhabitant of our spacious two-bedroom. I swore I felt her some nights, in the darkened, less-used spaces of our home. There is, in love, a certain kind of possession that takes place. We think our lovers belong to us, and so we think we own their pasts, as well. Pete's lingered thick in the air, irresistible.

So, one November morning, after Pete had left for work, I set out to find the hidden letters. It was cold in the apartment and still dark outside. Maybe there was the sound of rain falling, and the old apartment's frame groaning under the wind. But despite the dull cold, something welled up in me that felt like guilt and exhilaration, like those first moments Pete and I had shared.

I started in the street-facing spare bedroom that doubled as Pete's music practice space and my sewing room. In it sat a small desk with drawers squeaky and unaligned. One by one, I went through them, hoping to find the letters. I found his passport, an address book, and a metronome that let out a low, electronic whine when I turned it on. But no letters. On a nearby bookshelf were binders of jazz scores and song charts from bands Pete had played in. But no letters. Beneath the desk, in the space where someone's feet should have been, was a small cardboard box. Inside, I found old receipts and a birthday card I'd made him, and—finally, something unfamiliar—a large craft-paper envelope with his old address written on the outside in blue ink. It was postmarked Leipzig, Germany. I hesitated before opening it, although the flap had already been carefully unsealed.

The condition of the envelope told me its contents had been valued. Its brown paper was slightly wrinkled, soft to the touch, as if it had been opened and closed many times, or as if it had lived under a pillow for many nights. I opened it gingerly. My hands shook, and it crossed my mind that I should lock the door, should Pete have forgotten his umbrella or keys and return, interrupting my pathetic interlude with his past.

When I slid the envelope's contents out into my lap, I was surprised to find only four letters and a few photographs. Nonetheless, they seemed incredibly heavy, each of these letters in different-colored envelopes, written in fountain pen. I began reading the first one, but its contents were mundane: talk of dance performances and Charlotte's master's thesis, classical music recommendations. I began skimming. Where was the talk of love, of longing? All of the letters were signed "Love," of course, but this was their only romantic language.

But the pictures, as daybreak crept through the windows, grew brighter and more insistent, asking to be looked at. Save for that old black-and-white portrait, now slightly creased and mottled with fingerprints, they were all of her dancing. I was drawn to the curves of her body in a pink leotard and taffeta skirt. She had a slender neck, a small waist, a dancer's muscular legs and misshapen feet, toes pointed in midair. The same long, lithe arms that I had pictured pulling him into bed. There was a photo of Charlotte and Pete, standing in a train station, with a sign behind them: *Fahrkarten*. Tickets. She had her arm wrapped around his at the elbow, as if he were her dancing partner. As if about to spin him into an unforeseen pirouette—to take him by surprise and return the affection he had secretly harbored for her.

Behind the pictures was a small notebook with a black cover. I opened it. It was a calendar, with just a few etchings in it, Pete's handwriting. For his first few days in Germany, it appeared, he had kept an abbreviated diary. Each page, at the top, was numbered with a date—in European format, I noted: date first, month second. As I had suspected, there was talk of walking arm-in-arm. Talk of revealing a love that couldn't be. I wondered whether the impossibility was on account of the ocean that lay between them, but hoped it was on account of me.

After the first few entries, there were dates written atop the pages, but nothing else. As if those were the pages that would have held those things he kept just for himself, and as if they were so fragile that by being written, they would disappear. But I had found what I wanted: some record of the thrill he felt in those first days, when everything becomes memorable simply because it happened.

Charlotte had the benefit, in her relationship with Pete, that I never would: She and Pete would always be in those first stages of love, doomed—or maybe privileged—never to progress to the mundane. She would always remain enigmatic, to both Pete and me, for what we didn't know about her. Maybe Charlotte, like me, plays with her bottom lip when she's nervous. Maybe she, too, forgets to water houseplants. Maybe she leaves dirty dishes in the sink. But Pete will never know that about her, and therefore, she'll always remain a romantic ideal, someone whose image remains untarnished by what happens when we really get to know someone. And I'm still not sure which is better: to know our loves, or to remain in the bliss of not knowing them.

I put the letters back, careful to keep them in order, careful to close the flap gently. I tucked the brown envelope back in the cardboard box, right where it had been, and wandered down the long hallway, dazed. Without thinking, I reached atop a tall bookshelf and pulled down the small box that contained every letter I'd ever written Pete. The box itself had been a gift to him, a small antique trunk I'd found in disrepair and had spent weeks stripping and repainting, fitting with a new paper lining. The glossy red paint had gathered a layer of dust on top, and I brushed it off with my palm. The box was so full of letters that its top didn't close; I opened it the rest of the way and set it down next to me on the couch.

Here were my letters, hundreds of them. They were in no order, but I remembered their chronology by the color of their envelopes.

I first opened the early ones. Reading of my new love for him, even in my own words, felt like I was reading about a romance that wasn't mine. These words—my words, I had to remind myself—were laden with affection for him, affection I wasn't sure whether Charlotte had ever returned. I read each letter and let them all pile up in my lap afterward, envelopes neatly closed and facing the same way. It was the weight of them I liked, balanced on my knees such that, any moment, they might fall.

SO WOULD I STRIP YOUR TRAPPINGS OFF

Chicago, Illinois, 2006

I knew nothing about refinishing antiques when the miniature trunk arrived on my Chicago doorstep, in the spring of 2006, just three months before I would move to Oregon. I had ordered it off eBay from a seller who didn't know anything of its history or age. But after I had opened the shipping box, puncturing its tight tape with my house key, I cradled the lovely old thing and set out to trace its history, if only so that I could know what I would soon destroy with my sandpaper and paint. It was about a foot long and eight inches tall, a miniature replica of the steamer trunks used to carry nineteenth-century travelers' clothes on trans-Atlantic journeys. Its varnish was worn at the corners and on the rounded top. A leather band that circled the trunk was only half-attached. I opened the trunk and blew a layer of dust from the bottom. The paper lining, a pastel floral print yellowed by time and acid glue, was curled at the edges. I tugged a corner, testing the strength of the fixative that remained. The paper flaked between my fingers.

It turns out, I learned from the website of a trunk restorer in North Carolina, that this was called a "Western Squares doll trunk." Its exterior would once have been covered in brown paper crossed with thick, black lines, the Western Squares pattern that first emerged in the 1870s. The trunk was intended for little girls, to store a doll's wardrobe. Manufacturers used young girls' envy of their mothers' trunks to market these smaller versions. The Mendel-Drucker Trunk Company in Cincinnati, Ohio, had this imprint on the labels that adorned its doll trunks: "Like the Big Ones We Make for Mother."

On the trunk in question, only a few ragged fragments of the Western Squares paper remained, but the glue had stayed behind in broad swaths. The leather band that wrapped around the lid's edge had a small metal lock, now darkened by rust and patina. Had there once been a key? The lid's hinges, in the back, were blackened, too, but still sound. They would not need to be replaced, simply polished. I reveled in this and other ambitions, in the way I always bask in the possibility of a new art project. I like the hope inherent in what's not yet started, the anticipation for what it will be, more than I can ever love the fulfillment, the finished object. But this project was laced, too, with another form of expectation: It would be a gift for Pete, whose birthday was just a few weeks away. It would become a home for the stacks of letters I'd written him over the past four years, as if to say, "Keep them. Live, as I do, in our past." It is easier, I've learned, to view the past as ideal when we view it from a distance.

* * *

I met Pete when I was a senior at Northwestern, near Chicago, but living in San Francisco and interning to fulfill my journalism school requirements. I had returned to Chicago for the weekend, for a friend's twenty-first birthday. A group of us had gathered before dinner at my friend's apartment to watch her open gifts, and two college boys, music majors, had shown up with their gift "wrapped" in an empty Pabst Blue Ribbon beer box. But the gift itself was thoughtful: a collection of their favorite jazz CDs, tucked neatly in vinyl sleeves. I was intrigued enough to offer them a ride down to the Gold Coast neighborhood, where our group would have dinner. On weekends, the streets of this posh neighborhood were packed with parked cars. We circled the blocks, around Schiller and Goethe streets, Division and Wells, finding nothing. The afternoon snow that had fallen didn't help; it seemed all the people who lived here were in for the night, their windows a yellowed, vellum warm as we rounded corners in the cold outside. Finally, we saw a spot. I was stopped, prepared to slide in, when we saw the sign, askance in a snowdrift as if struck by a wayward plow or bumper: Loading Zone, 15 Feet. Without speaking, or that's how I remember it, Pete and his friend Evan climbed from the car at the same time. Feet steadied in the snow, they tugged at the sign pole till the frozen ground gave way. The gall! I laughed from the driver's seat as they one-two-three heaved the offending sign into a neighbor's front shrubbery. I didn't get a ticket.

At the restaurant, a sushi place lit in dim blues, our group sat at a long, narrow table. I found myself at the end, with these sign-slinging college guys on either side of me. I admit I paid little attention to Pete; in fact, I remember him being there only as his friend Evan's accomplice. After I flew back to San Francisco, I sent letters to Evan, accompanied by funny clips from the newspaper or *The New Yorker*, appealing to what little I knew of his quick, cynical wit. The letters let our friendship take hold: When I returned to Northwestern for spring semester, Evan welcomed me into his crowd of friends, members of a rock band who sat playing instruments in an attic and drinking cheap beer. I liked these guys for all sorts of unexpected reasons: their torn-up khaki pants, their dirty jokes, their talk of Stravinsky's symphonies and Chekhov's stories under the single, exposed bulb of the attic on Pratt Street. I tried my first and only ecstasy with them, a crushed-up pill I snorted clumsily through a rolled dollar bill. Later that same night, Pete and I found ourselves in the attic alone, though we had no expectations for romance. Instead, he plucked single notes on his electric bass and, as if emboldened by the unshaded bulb, or the attic's slanted roof pushing in on me, pushing the words out, I began mumbling some kind of spoken-word poetry. Something welled up in me, in the synchrony, and we kept going on momentum alone, on the key changes and the prolonged notes.

Within days, we had kissed. I remember the last word I'd said, before he pulled me in: "chemistry." I was talking about the class. But the word lingered as his arm slid around me and my face slanted toward his. I was too aware of the moment, of the fact that the word worked doubly. I think I will, forever, seek this feeling of firstness. I would move away, write letters, visit. With each return, there was a sliver of what wasn't there rearriving. Each time I left, I created for myself the sense of longing I craved. I wanted, always, a nostalgia that couldn't exist when Pete and I were together, geographically. I nurtured opportunities to long for him, to write sentimental letters that traveled across states. Maybe that's why, for the next ten years, I would leave Pete many times, putting distance between us just to bridge it with my own words. Or, I consider now, I left so many times not because I wanted to return, but because I was trying to figure out how to leave him for good, even if I could not have named the reason.

I always thought I sought the easy initiation of our first night, the kissing night, when Pete had pulled away and said, "It's late. Why don't you stay." A statement, not a question. After that first one, our nights together continued—nights when he would play Mahler's First Symphony on CD as we fell asleep. In the spaces between notes, between movements, he explained to me how the alive springtime of the first movement betrayed the minor interpretation of the old French nursery rhyme "Frère Jacques" in the third, turned a child's tune to a funeral march in the downward shift of a few notes. These nights, in my memory, are awash in dark music that pulled me in, that gave love's initial giddiness a new gravity, a sense of lasting.

* * *

The first letter I wrote to Pete was only a few months after the January we'd met, only a couple of weeks after those first few nights with him.

The letter I wrote wasn't, in fact, a letter at all. The goal was a silly one: to ask him to my sorority's formal dance, approaching just a couple of weeks away. Normally, this would have been done in passing, over a drink after Friday's last class. But the newness of this, Pete's constant presence in my mind, called for something better. So I walked to downtown Evanston, a short stroll away from the manicured campus, and went to the Saville flower shop. Here was my idea: a bunch of tulips, each tagged with a different reason why I wanted him to accompany me to this dance, but more largely, why I loved him, though I surely wasn't ready to say so.

Tulips in hand, I walked back to my sorority house room and

104

called my friend Kate, an artist, aesthete, and hopeless romantic whose enthusiasm would, I knew, harden my nerves to the task ahead. Kate was there in minutes, and we spent the afternoon cutting circles from multicolored paper, affixing ribbons to them. On each of the circles, I wrote, in painstaking calligraphy, a reason, a "because" phrase: "Because I look cute in your clothes." "Because I need to loosen up." "Because someone else loves driving toward the Chicago skyline as much as I do." "Because shoes aren't always necessary, nor is an agenda," and finally, "Because the best dances are in moonlight and to no music," referring to our penchant for stopping in empty streets on our way home late at night, dancing on the double yellow line, taking turns humming Tom Waits tunes. Kate and I tied one tag to each tulip. And then, binding them all together with another ribbon, I hung a larger tag: "I am asking you to Delta Gamma formal because . . ." I gingerly wrapped a damp paper towel around the flowers' stems to keep them from wilting.

The day was one of the first that signaled spring: a slight lifting of the cold, the sun soaking into our skin. Tulips in hand, I climbed into Kate's Jetta. It was the first windows-down day of the season, or we made it so despite the lingering chill. Kate was always blasting music, silly pop that I secretly loved. Today, it was Enrique Iglesias, and we sang together in a way only spring can bring on: "You can run, you can hide, but you can't escape my love." It was a short drive to the music building, where certainly we'd find Pete in one of the windowless practice rooms that filled the building with discord, with orchestral anarchy. But as we approached Regenstein Hall, I panicked. At the front door, I thrust the flowers into Kate's hand. "Here, you do it."

I was hiding in the women's bathroom when Kate extracted me by one arm. Pete was waiting outside the door. "Of course," he said, though there hadn't been a question to answer. He was wearing pajamas, messed-up hair, and his easy smile. I remember the welling up of something inside me, something I didn't know. Not until now would I question this other sensibility: that it was the feeling I loved, more than the person, and that I would pursue this feeling for as long as we would be together.

* * *

Among my favorite stores in Chicago is the Paper Source, housed in an old, three-story Victorian just west of downtown, a few blocks from the famous Magnificent Mile shopping district. This store is warm inside and well-lit, its contents a sea of colors. So I delighted in the opportunity to go there as I began imagining what the old trunk could become, remade in my vision. I pictured something Art Deco: high-gloss red paint on the outside, patterned paper glued in a careful layer over the interior.

The Paper Source has a broad display of oversized, patterned papers, hanging on rods similar to the ones libraries use to hold the day's newspapers. These racks cover one whole wall of the store, floor to ceiling, front to back. I lingered before the choices. There were Japanese silkscreens, Indian block prints, vellums so thin and translucent I could see my fingers through them as I rubbed their edges, papers with real leaves and flowers pressed into them. But I was choosing for Pete, so my romantic tendencies toward real flora and rounded shapes wouldn't do. Instead, I focused my attention on a section of geometric prints—hard lines, unyielding squares. And that's where I saw a red-and-green print on off-white paper—decidedly Deco. It reminded me of the Frank Lloyd Wright and Louis Sullivan glass patterns we'd seen on display at the Art Institute, of the slightly curvaceous geometry of the historic buildings Pete and I had snuck through on self-guided tours. I extracted the sheet gingerly from its rack.

I have always reveled in having just the right materials to complete any art project. In art, there is no making do for me. There is no substitute for just the right felt-tip pen, eraser, or pair of scissors. Cotton embroidery floss won't work where wool is called for; Elmer's glue won't take the place of acid-free polyvinyl adhesive. I pride myself on having a vast collection of art supplies, each procured as a project called for it. Now, in my house in New Mexico, I have my own art room—the second bedroom in a small apartment. The room houses broad baskets of stacked fabrics and balled-up yarn, rotary quilt cutters and mats called "self-healing" because they are not scarred by the strokes of an X-Acto knife. There are baskets of multi-colored paper and blank greeting cards, boxes each labeled with their contents: Glues and Tapes, Bookbinding Supplies, Stamps and Ink, Punches and Embossers.

Back at home in my Chicago apartment, however, my hopes for the letter box were quickly quieted. An Internet search on removing paper and glue from old wood offered more cautionary tales than suggestions: The wood might warp. It might crack under the pressure of sanding. It might be moldy beneath the paper covering. But barring any of these circumstances, I should use some combination—it wasn't quite clear—of wetting the paper, scraping it off with a spackling knife, and sanding. At the urging of these websites, these masters of furniture refinishing, I began to doubt myself, began to think that maybe the trunk couldn't be preserved—and neither, then, could my letters.

* * *

In the fall of 2003, I was again living in San Francisco. I'd moved back a few months earlier—nearly a year, exactly, after the kissing day that cemented Pete and me. Though I claimed it was just a change of scenery I was craving, better weather, a home near the ocean, I suspect now that it was distance I wanted, distance that would allow me to miss Pete. I don't think I realized it then, for I had never left a lover before, never even had a significant relationship, but I would come to know how separation gives rise to a longing stronger, almost, than our initial love, than those first nights with Mahler and talking in the dark between the notes. And my distance would ask of Pete the same longing. So I left—packed just the important possessions in the back of my Toyota and drove across the country, stopping along the way for nights in Boulder, in Salt Lake City, going to concerts in these strange, mountainous towns and wishing someone were there to explain the music to me.

As I remember it, my time in San Francisco was an endless string of letters to Pete. I'm sure there was more to it, but when memories are long enough in the past, we distill them to their most concentrated form, and my memories lie in the letters I wrote, near-nightly. It was as if I lived there not for myself, but to tell Pete what I was doing, to create the illusion of an independence that, in the end, was subverted by my need to share every bit of it via the mail. I lived in a studio apartment in Hayes Valley, where I turned my large but windowless walk-in closet into an art room. I moved in a desk and swivel chair, used the shelves intended for sweaters and shoes to store boxes of art supplies, instead. Each night, I sat down in my closet and began a letter to Pete. I lived my life as a series of memories in the making, less important in themselves than in how I would relay them, an anticipation that led me like a forward-slanting shadow as I traversed the city's hilly terrain, sat by its bay eating takeout hamburgers from Red's Java House, and lounged alone in its dark bars, dragging on cigarettes and exhaling toward low ceilings stained a warm, parchment yellow.

Buying the paper for the inside of the letter box had been the easy part, the fun part. But given the online instructions I'd read, I needed to add more than art supplies to my arsenal. During my lunch break the next day, I walked to the hardware store and emerged with a broad, flat putty knife and sandpaper in three different grains—coarse, medium, fine. Next, I stood in the paint section, amid racks of tiny cards in ROY-G-BIV order, holding cranberry reds next to pomegranate, cardinal against Red Delicious, persimmon flush with crimson. I chose the richest, most saturated red—like a child's balloon—and watched as the man behind the counter mixed up a small container, holding it beneath a sequence of spouts. Before hammering the can closed, he dropped a dollop of red on the lid, and I delighted in watching it dry as I walked back to my office, as if some part of the project were now visible in this small swatch of its hue.

Back at home, that evening, I set up my refurbishing station in the living room, well-lit by a broad bay window. I laid out newspaper over my craft table, soaked sponges under the faucet to prep them. With my instruments lined up like a surgeon's, I sized up the trunk. Everything I'd read advised me to wet the paper first, to see whether it would peel straight off after being soaked and rubbed with the sponge. Sure enough, much of it peeled off in damp clumps. But the glue beneath the stripped paper was stubborn. It wouldn't budge; it remained affixed to the trunk's domed lid. I waited for the wet wood to dry, to mend itself, before setting in with the sandpaper.

I started with coarse grain, rubbing at the glue until smooth wood emerged beneath it. I feared weathering away the entire surface of the trunk's lid, where the glue was especially persistent. But in time, the wood showed through. Dust rose in the air and alighted on nearby objects. I persisted, pulling my T-shirt up around my face. By evening's end, the old trunk was naked—bare of glue, paper, past, stripped of its history so that I could preserve my own.

* * *

That fall in San Francisco, the season of endless letters written in my closet, Pete came to visit. He was in town for a college friend's wedding celebration, which began on Friday night with a bonfire on Ocean Beach, the miles-long stretch of sand that runs the city's west edge. At night, hundreds of fires light up the coastline. They stretch along the shore like nodes, or single stars in a constellation. Pete taught me that night to find Orion. Look, he said, for the three stars of his belt. We found him, lying on his side, shooting his arrow upward from a bow we couldn't quite discern. I still look for Orion in the fall sky.

Among a circle of people drawn to the warmth of a fire, we both felt alone, gazing toward Orion, digging our hands into the cold, damp sand and each other's shoulders. We walked down to the shore, far enough from the fire that the susurrus of the waves at high tide overcame the voices from behind us and the crackle of new kindling tossed atop the flames. We rolled up our jeans, waded in, and despite our best efforts, emerged with wet, salty cuffs that clung to our ankles, that would grow stiff in the cold. When we returned to the fire, someone had turned on a small boom box, nearly inaudible over the voices and the sparks bursting open into the night. But Pete recognized a tune: "That's Leonard Cohen," he said. I knew nothing of him, except what I could discern: a low, gravelly voice punctuated by chimes—like regret, but not without hope.

When we decided to leave, it was so Pete could play Leonard Cohen for me. He had brought the CD with his collection. We

110

returned to my Hayes Street studio, tracking a trail of sand across the hardwood. We ordered a pizza. Forty-five minutes, they said. Enough time to shower—the white-hot steam rising and the sand swirling down the drain in dark trails between our feet—then to fall into my bed and listen to "Suzanne," to "Famous Blue Raincoat." The night had been cold, though we hadn't realized it until we'd crawled under layers of blankets to listen to Leonard sing, "That was called love for the workers in song, probably still is for those of them left." And as we lay on the bed, I felt myself not in the moment, then, but as if I were looking back on us from some point in the distant future, from what might as well be now. I was already longing. I wanted to long.

When he departed, days later, Pete left sand. I found it in the rolled-up cuffs of my jeans, the cracks of my shower tile, around the rim of a half-empty beer he'd abandoned in the fridge. Under my fingernails and in my hair. But he had taken Leonard Cohen, so that day, as nostalgia crept back in, I felt somehow fuller, fulfilled by the return of longing itself.

Every interval of togetherness has its antithesis, its corresponding episode of apartness. I think of these episodes like cairns, the piles of stones hikers plant for themselves at crucial forks on a path. If the hikers become lost, the cairns tell them how to get home. After living in San Francisco, I became restless. Whenever I thought Pete and I had grown too grounded, too comfortable, bordering on complacent, I skipped town, returned us to the life of longing, distance, of letters. In the years since San Francisco, I have moved to Oregon, Chicago, Missouri, and now New Mexico. I realize that I left, all those times, only to nurture nostalgia, to prolong longing. It is longing that I like best; for once it's fulfilled, what are we left to desire?

Perhaps that's why I am in constant backward pursuit of love's newness: Is newness not marked by the presence of constant longing for the other, longing that dissipates with actual, lived-out togetherness? Much of the appeal in those deliberate distances came from writing letters, from a fabricated sense of nostalgia. Letters are a physical embodiment of absence; for we write the letter to stand in for ourselves, as body metonymy. My inaugural act, upon arriving in a place, was always to write Pete a letter, as if the very doing so confirmed—was my own solid evidence—that I had arrived.

* * *

In the end, the longing I'd so relished had overpowered me: I moved back to Chicago after just nine months in San Francisco. Closing the distance would, I thought, resolve the deliberate space I'd taken care to put between us. While I was packing up the Hayes Valley studio, Pete found us a crumbling, sunlit apartment near Wrigley Field, a place where comfort, but complacency, too, came on quick and hung thick in the air after just a few months. After a year together in that apartment, we had seen our undoing in the works for a while, but Pete had initiated the words in his silence, had told me we were done. It wasn't that any one event had destroyed us; rather, we'd eroded over time, losing sand-size grains with each small fight, each night he slept on the couch, each time I left the dishes in the sink to grow crusty and smelly. It was this accumulation of sand that built up in the bottom of the hourglass until all we had left was the knowledge that staying had been easier than leaving.

In the previous days, Pete had been evasive, avoiding talking in the way he always did when he was deciding something, figuring out how to put words to what had been left unsaid for so long. So I knew it was inevitable, and something in the air that morning told me that the day had come, that he'd found his words. He sat on the couch, watching baseball, his acoustic guitar propped across his lap. The announcer's voice on the television was punctuated by occasional, elegiac chords Pete strummed, chords that never came together to make a song, but instead, sat singly in the air, lingering and long.

I sat in the craft room, composing him a letter. We had just rearranged this room. Previously, it had been Pete's music room, housing the noble upright bass whose neck reached almost to the ceiling, and a host of smaller instruments: acoustic guitars, an acoustic bass, an electric bass made of dark, sturdy babinga and wenge woods. My crafts had been relegated to the kitchen table, where I often left string, markers, and turpentine tins strewn about. On account of my messiness, we had not eaten dinner at the kitchen table in months, instead plopping down on the couch with plates in our laps, chewing in silence, eyes fixed on the TV. I resented that Pete had a space for his art, and that I was forced to usurp spaces in the apartment for my own, making it more a burden than something to be admired. I had told him this, and one afternoon, we moved the kitchen table into the music room, and all my boxes and crates of art supplies with it. The basses, then, came into the kitchen. This, I thought, would make things better just by making them different. Nothing had changed, though. We still couldn't eat at the kitchen table. I still left dirty dishes in the sink and art supplies strewn about.

So, on a June afternoon a year after I'd returned to Chicago for Pete, I sat in my newly appointed craft room, a host of blank cards and markers spread out on the former kitchen table. Pete had not said anything, yet, but I was already writing him a goodbye letter with an epilogue from the poet Mark Strand. *We have done what we wanted,* Strand writes in "Coming to This." *We have discarded dreams, preferring the heavy industry of each other.* I didn't know it at the time, but these words would be my crutch, my only possible way of remaining composed when the time did come. For letters, in that sense, are a sort of betrayal. They are planned, rehearsed, revised, a neat and tidy means of expression that belies the real urge: to cry, scream, shout, act on instinct alone. Indeed, this letter, in its calm voice, concealed how I really was. I tried writing Strand's poem, but my hands shook. I ended up typing it (a defeat), printing it out, and gluing it to the back of a postcard.

> *Coming to this*
> *has its rewards: nothing is promised, nothing is taken away.*
> *We have no heart or saving grace,*
> *no place to go, no reason to remain.*

The same went for the letter that accompanied it; I could not write, so I typed—more defeat. I finished it with the words "The End," as if this were Aesop's lost fable. I tucked the postcard and printed letter together in a pale pink envelope, struggled to write just the four-letter name on the outside. When I gave it to him, he read it and simply nodded. I had done his job for him.

* * *

After he left, Pete was staying on friends' couches and occasionally in the passenger seat of his white Honda Civic, parked on a nearby street. He would come over on Saturday afternoons with a couple of empty boxes or plastic milk crates and fill them item by item in slow, stolid movements that indicated even he questioned whether this choice was right. Once, he packed a few things—bass cords, coffee mugs, a ceramic Buddha I'd always wondered why he kept in the first place—and then simply lay on the floor next to his half-empty box. He buried his face in the blue Berber rug, and I could see how he shook, so the only thing left to do was to lie down next to him, to put my arm around him and run my fingers through his hair, which had a familiar, soft oiliness to it. We stayed that way until it felt like something was better, though I suspect neither of us could have said what, except that we remembered the past as better than it had been.

Eventually, his things were gone and Pete was staying at the apartment of a few friends, just a six-block walk from where I lived. I knew that his bicycle was parked out back, chained to the fence. I think it was that knowledge alone, that piece of knowing where some part of him was, that made me want to write the letter. The letter was nothing special: "I miss having someone to laugh with daily." The idea was so hurried and its execution so urgent that it was simple in design: A piece of paper torn from a spiral notebook, tucked into a cellophane envelope, in case of rain. I punched a hole in the envelope and strung through it a loop of green ribbon large enough to slide onto the bike's handlebar.

I walked the letter over as night fell, took the alley behind Eddy Street to our friends' apartment. Sure enough, there was Pete's bike. I had to be careful, though, for I knew the back gate had a sensor that would trigger an automatic floodlight if I stepped in the wrong direction. Not that I was doing anything wrong. But still, the move felt like it should be surreptitious, stealthy, like this admission that I missed him must be kept secret until it was revealed by the letter. I slipped it onto his bike, then slinked back through the alley, out to the street.

I went after that to a bar around the corner, one my friends frequented. As I walked, I began to regret my decision, in the same way anything done under cover of night seems shameful, regrettable, no matter how good the intentions. I could, I reasoned, duck back into the alley and recover the letter. But I didn't. Instead, I pushed through the two sets of doors that held the air conditioning in at the Southport, a divey old place with a padded blue-vinyl bar. There sat Pete, paging through a thick book but not really reading, I could tell. He had a half-finished pitcher of beer in front of him, apparently one he'd ordered just for himself. Here's where my sneaking continued, as I stepped up quietly behind him, and without saying anything, put my hand on his shoulder. When he turned around to face me, he seemed to know whom to expect; his countenance didn't question, it accepted me, drew me in. I sat down.

"Fancy meeting you here," I said.

I looked more closely at his book: It was the A–L volume of a condensed encyclopedia. The bar had a shelf of books in a back corner, and I suspected M–Z was over there, somewhere. He had folded the book over his hand before I could see what he was reading: Albatross, perhaps? Alaska? I asked for a glass and filled it for myself from Pete's pitcher. I'm not sure what we talked about, only this coincidence: That morning, leaving my apartment for work, I had found a box of blank notecards sitting atop a garbage bin in the alley. What a waste, I thought, and picked them up. Certainly, someone had put them there, instead of in the bin, for the benefit of some passerby. So I had these notecards in my purse, and while Pete was on Aluminum or Austria, I wrote him a card: "It is good to share my favorite lines from a new book, good to feel comfortable in words and no words at all. Good to study the lines of your profile and remember the softly wrought lines of a love." I handed it to him, and he read it right there. Letters are a bit uncanny, I realize now. They're our way of revealing what ought not to be revealed, or what we're afraid to say in person. But being in someone's company while they read our letters, read the words that are, by their nature, unspoken, is awkward, just as embarrassing as if we had said the words rather than written them. We hide behind the pen in a letter, behind rehearsal and artifice and persona. But there we are, ultimately, looking the object of our desire straight in the eye.

Pete stayed at the old apartment that night, fit easily back into his dent that remained on the right side of the bed, the side that abutted the wall. And it was as it had always been: By morning, we had rolled from our dents to meet in the center.

* * *

After sanding the trunk bare, I had filled its cracks with wood filler, primed it to make sure the high-gloss paint would shine. I paused, then. Painting has always instilled in me a certain trepidation, as if in one faulty stroke, I could bring a project to its undoing. I decided to test the paint on a stray piece of wood that had made its way into my bin of art project debris, the cast-offs that served no other purpose than to be tested on, messed up. And sure enough, this shade was a vibrant hot pink. Not child's balloon, not fire engine, not persimmon, even. It was the shade of the ugliest geraniums. I drove to the nearest hardware store, insisted upon the reddest red. The dollop of paint on the can's lid proved it would be.

* * *

One year after our breakup, by the summer of 2006, Pete had found a more permanent home—an apartment on Chicago's northwest side. We were still "friends," our parlance for frequent nights out that, occasionally, ended up in one of us spending the night at the other's place; that ended up in our falling asleep to Mahler; that ended up in the familiar feel of his skin and the way the oils of his hair made my fingertips smell sweet, with the faintest trace of onions. Meanwhile, the letters had continued to accumulate, most of them restrained versions of the longing I had actually felt.

About a month after I'd started it, the box was nearly finished. Coated in two layers of the reddest red paint, the trunk was beginning to look as I had imagined. It shone; light beaded in small circles on its rounded top. I applied the paper lining, measuring, cutting the broad sheet of expensive paper in perfect sizes, fearful of missing a corner or overshooting an edge. I used a foam brush to apply acid-free glue to the back of each piece, pressed it into place, smoothed it down with the flat side of a river rock to get the bubbles out. And I let it dry, let it age in its own way, come into comfort with its new trappings.

When I took the box to Pete, it was his birthday. Pete's bedroom in his new apartment was hardly furnished—a mattress on the floor, a series of stacked milk crates for bookshelves—so it was easy to spot the letters. He had moved them all to one place, a yellow-flannel drawstring bag that had originally housed a set of sheets we'd bought. The sheets had long ago been discarded, having developed holes at one end where Pete's toes had dug right through. This old, leftover bag full of letters was tucked behind the bedroom door.

I had told him I was coming over, but he was sleeping. Quietly, I reached into the corner behind his door and removed the yellow bag full of letters. By this point, they had outgrown their home, the corners of envelopes straining the bag's seams and peeking out from its drawstring top. One by one, I removed them and stacked them in the box. It was, I see now, my way of urging him to save the letters. I was tempted to open each one, to relive its contents, but I feared the sound of shuffling papers would awaken Pete. I looked over at him as I accomplished this stealthy task, watched his eyebrows twitch in some dream.

When I'd finished, I laid a hand on one shoulder to rouse him. He opened his eyes with a knowing look, not surprise.

"Happy birthday, darlin'," I said—"darlin'" always the parlance of love.

He grumbled and stirred, put his hand atop my own. I was sitting on the edge of his mattress, holding the box in my lap. When he saw it, he sat up and took it into his hands.

"This is beautiful," he murmured. "How did you do this?"

His bewildered amazement was exactly the reaction I'd wanted, hoped for in my time spent sanding, filling cracks, polishing old hinges. As he removed the letters, eager to see the inside of the trunk, I handed him a final, new one: a card bearing Amy Lowell's poem "Aubade," handwritten in careful, swirling letters:

> *As I would free the white almond from the green husk*
> *So would I strip your trappings off,*
> *Beloved.*
> *And fingering the smooth and polished kernel*
> *I should see that in my hands glittered a gem beyond counting.*

Surrounded by piles of multicolored envelopes addressed in my painstaking script, I explained my process, showed him pictures I'd taken of each step. With the trunk's old life, its peeling Western Squares paper, juxtaposed with this shiny, red new one, I felt a different sort of longing: not for what had already transpired between us, but for what would come. I longed for the letters that would come to fill this box, to overflow it and peek from its top, so that the shiny brass clasp wouldn't close, no matter how we tried.

THE TWO OF US, DANCERS

Columbia, Missouri, 2010

There we were, suddenly, as if shoved by the force of winter wind, in a room full of square dancers. The lights were hot-yellow overhead in this storefront on our humble Missouri town's main drag. The space had once housed an art gallery, but its fixtures and sculptures were now replaced by a rowdy roomful of young dancers in thick-ruffled skirts, plaid shirts and suspenders. The music, fast and twangy, echoed off the walls and wood floors, punctuated by the click of cowboy boots and the commands of the dance caller, a man with a headset microphone and a beard that touched his belt buckle. The room smelled of sweat and booze, and the plate glass windows were fogged with warmth.

We—my friend Anya, her husband, and I—were not supposed to be here. In our black, dressy clothes, the three of us had come from an art gallery reception and were headed to dinner just a few doors down. But as we walked past the spectacle, Anya peered in, then opened the door just a crack to let the room's cacophony slip out into the cold. And when she stepped in, or rather, danced in, Anya's husband and I had followed her. Neither of us could resist Anya's whims, not even someone shy like I am, someone who would never enter a room filled with strangers just because they were dancing.

But to Anya, this was no deterrent. So while Steven and I lingered by the door, awaiting our quick escape, Anya two-stepped and do-si-doed, laughing at her own uneven beat.

"Tantsuyte, Lena!"—*Dance, Lena!* she said, calling me by my Russian nickname, reaching out to grab my elbow. But I was stealthy and stepped back, pinned myself against the window.

"Nyet," I said. "Ya ne tantsuyu." That I don't dance wasn't quite true. I just dance horribly.

This would not, I suspect, have mattered to Anya. She just wanted a dancing partner, someone who would join her in the perpetual motion she seemed to be in, not only that night, but always. Anya dances through life, as if always in midair, in the moment between her feet leaving the ground and touching back down.

* * *

I met her shortly after beginning my PhD program in Missouri. Along with my English coursework, I had decided to enroll in Russian-language courses. My reasons were, admittedly, farfetched: I had recently begun to attempt lace knitting—in particular, large, triangle-shaped shawls with complicated eyelet patterns. I marveled at one particular type, called "Orenburg lace shawls" for the Russian region where they originated. The patterns of their rural knitters, it was said, could not be replicated by knitters anywhere else. They make shawls so gossamer, it's fabled, one can slide them through a wedding ring. It sounded romantic to me, this legend of patterns passed down but never shared outside Orenburg. I longed to work not from English translations, but from the real patterns, many of them passed down through generations. I pined to someday go to Orenburg, to see for myself this region of mythic knitting.

Anya, who had come from St. Petersburg for a master's degree in Russian literature, was the teaching assistant in my Russian class. As a teacher, she made the Russian language sing in the same way that she danced around the room, always dynamic, never afraid to laugh at herself. She seemed to delight in teaching us slang—for example, that the Russian word for "sausage"—*kol'basa*—can also be used to refer to a wild party. She told anecdotes about how elevators ("lifts," she called them) are forever out of order in Russia, so that she and several friends had once been trapped in one, with a melting ice-cream cake for a birthday party, for two hours. When the word for "eggs"—*yaytsa*—appeared on our vocabulary list, she simply cautioned, "Be very careful with this word," smiling to herself. It turns out, I later learned, it's also slang for testicles.

Occasionally, I would speak to Anya after class, our relationship a bit different, more collegial, given I was the only graduate student in the course and we were close in age, she thirty-one and I thirty at the time. But I confess, I was intimidated by her—not only the contagious energy, but the beauty that accompanied it: her small face, hazel eyes, and choppy blonde hair. Anya seemed so naturally self-assured that I was certain—in the way women create hierarchies for themselves—that she was too good for me, that my admiration for her was unreciprocated.

But one day in late winter—in my second semester as Anya's

student—I was packing up my books at the end of class when she came over to me. She reached out her hand and ran it over the shawl I was wearing. I had knitted it myself—my first lace triangle, though it was made with worsted-weight wool, hardly gossamer or delicate, not at all like the shawls of Orenburg. Suddenly my face felt flushed on account of Anya's attention, her fingers wrapped in the fabric of my scarf.

"Oh, Lena," she said, "you have to teach me how to knit." I still recall the intonation in her voice when she said this, the slow longing it evoked. And I knew that this wasn't one of Anya's whims—for even without knowing her well, I sensed her whimsy—but something she really did want. So I agreed to come to her office hours the next day.

That afternoon, I went home and selected the most beautiful materials from my collection: a skein of my favorite merino wool yarn in a soft green the color of rosebuds before they've opened and a set of bamboo needles not too big but not too small, easily maneuvered in a beginner's hands. I reveled in this first step, in the chance to pass on the choreography of casting on, knitting, and purling to someone else. I sensed, too, that it could become the beginning of the friendship I'd wanted to form with Anya, but hadn't known how to. But Anya had asked for my help, and I hoped I could do more than teach her to knit; it felt as if I had been asked to share a secret. I hoped I could show her that knitting is not just needles and yarn and stitch patterns. It is tactile, sensual, the beauty of its materials something that must be pursued to really be appreciated. It is the sound of two people crossing paths in a lonely late-night alley.

I showed up the next day at her office hours, as we'd planned. I had arrived with my carefully selected yarn and needles, a magazine of knitting patterns for Anya to choose from, and *The Complete Idiot's Guide to Knitting and Crochet*, the book from which I'd taught myself to knit years earlier. Anya and another Russian instructor, Viktoria, sat in the cramped, warm office that smelled of stale coffee. I greeted them in Russian, but quickly switched to English.

"I brought the knitting supplies," I said. Noting that they were both hunched over piles of class assignments, grading, I added, "If you have time to learn."

I'll confess, in that moment, I doubted Anya's sincerity, got a bit flushed at the prospect that maybe she hadn't meant what she'd said at all, in spite of the conviction I thought her voice had held. My palms sweated as I lingered in the office doorway, waiting to be invited in.

I was relieved when Anya answered, "Konechno," *of course*, then pulled a chair with a ripped vinyl cushion into the center of the room for me.

I sat down and began pulling yarn and needles from my bag. I handed one set to Anya and one to Viktoria. I began to explain to them the first step, casting on stitches, but Anya quickly interrupted me.

"At Russian office hours, we speak in Russian," she said, not exactly sternly, but not with room for objection, either. I hesitated. For all my knitting knowledge, and for my modest Russian knowledge, I had no combination of the two: no Russian vocabulary to talk about knitting. The room felt suddenly warmer. My small hands shook as I put them over Anya's long, nimble fingers, guiding her through the first row of stitches. I became flustered and stumbled through even simple sentences, used to only the speaking drills and rehearsed dialogues we did in class, but not accustomed to having to narrate my thoughts on the fly or to explain the complexities of knitting. Just as I felt confident as a knitter—enough, finally, to trust that I could teach someone else to love it as I did—I was reduced again to a beginner. My hands could maneuver the stitches, could position the yarn between Anya's fingers, but I struggled to explain what I was doing or why. Anya, though, was patient with me. She supplied the vocabulary I lacked, terms she knew as a native speaker, even as a non-knitter. I wrote them down in a small notebook, the words for to knit, to purl, stitch, row, needles, yarn, gauge, and tension. She seemed to understand that this was harder for me than it was for her, that to begin anything—again or for the first time—makes anyone uncertain. But as I sat beside her, shaping her hands around the needles, showing her how to turn her small sample square after each row, her calmness relaxed me, and it felt, somehow, as if her firm, sturdy hands were steadying mine.

After this first lesson, after my flustered Russian explanations and my shaky hands joined with Anya's, a sort of covert hand-holding I'd longed for, I would never have guessed that in a few months, Anya would steady me again and again, would restore calm to my life, after Pete left.

* * *

A few lessons later, Anya could cast on stitches without my help and knit on double-pointed needles—not a complicated task, but a daunting one, since the knitter must manage four or five needles at once. Despite her repeated lament, "I can't do anything with my hands," or her Russian outburst "Ya armageddon!"—*I'm a disaster!*—Anya was a fast learner and a coordinated knitter. I trust she came to it naturally because she had grown up around knitting. Her mother used to knit as a side profession, taking commissions to make sweaters, hats, scarves, and socks for friends, family, and neighbors. Anya told me, sadly, that her mom doesn't knit anymore because her eyesight is poor, and I think in some small way, Anya wanted to knit to make up for what her mother could no longer do, to carry on a family tradition that otherwise would have ended a generation before her. When Anya had finished her first gauge swatch—a small square made to measure the number of stitches per inch—I told her she could unravel it; it was just a test. But she said, "Can I keep it? I want to show it to my mother."

Anya told me that same day, laughing, that she had always wanted her mother to be a street sweeper.

"Why?" I asked.

"Because then she could walk around Saint Petersburg all day, keeping it beautiful," she answered. "But she never did become a street sweeper." Instead, she was a knitter, and I think Anya found equal merit in that occupation. For early on, she would take home my yarn and needles to practice, and when she arrived to teach my class, would bring her swatch with her, eagerly showing me what she'd done, running it between her fingers in the characteristic way Anya had of touching everything, marveling at its tactility.

* * *

About a month into our knitting lessons, Anya and I were still meeting once or twice a week during her office hours, but we'd begun to spend time together outside the small Russian TA office, as well. First, there was the outing to the art gallery opening and to dinner when we stopped, impromptu, at the square dance. A couple of weeks later, ready to move past making stitch samples and on to a real project—a slouchy beret she had chosen from my pattern books—Anya asked me to help her pick out her first yarn. So one weekend afternoon, I picked up Anya at her house and drove her to the local yarn shop. It was not nearly so sophisticated and beautiful as my favorite Chicago store had been, in the hip neighborhood where I'd lived with Pete just a year earlier. This shop was one storefront in a strip mall, territory it shared with a vacuum

126

repair place and a shop that, mysterious for mid-Missouri, sold deep-sea diving gear. It was fluorescent-lit and carpeted in a drab shade of gray. Its walls, though, displayed rich-colored wools and soft, furry alpacas.

The proprietors never seemed to mind that, to choose between two skeins, I'd test their softness by picking them up and rubbing them over my cheek. Anya's temptation, I quickly saw, was the same as mine. She touched everything, picking up skeins and turning them over between her hands. Around the shop hung model garments—sample baby sweaters and scarves knit from the yarns for sale. Anya ran her fingers over every one. "Kak milyi," she said over and over—*how darling.* She leaned over a table filled with hand-painted ceramic buttons, picking up each one to examine it more closely. "Kak milyi." I hesitated to explain that we wouldn't need buttons for this hat pattern. Instead, I let her marvel at everything in the store, needed or not. I saw emerging in her my own love for these materials, saw the same excitement building in her that I know so well, that insatiable desire to begin something new. At last, Anya settled on fluffy red yarn made of blended alpaca and cashmere fibers. It was the perfect choice, I thought. "Kak milyi," I said to her.

* * *

As we continued our meetings, now working on the same hat pattern—hers red, mine from a skein of blue alpaca I'd been saving for something special—I continued to probe why this connection felt so easy, but also so important, born of something we both wanted and knew the other wanted without it ever being articulated. I wonder, now, whether we would have said it, had I known the words in Russian, or she in English—whether maybe that's why we didn't try so hard, and maybe that's why this succeeded: because we just let it be, without confining it to explanation.

Nonetheless, I tried to explain it to myself. One mid-February afternoon, after Anya and I had knitted and then we'd walked together toward her next class, I wrote this: "So, today, our quick walk and shouting Russian goodbyes to each other seemed to turn the late-winter air suddenly a shade warmer. 'Do piatnitsu,' (*Until Friday!*) I shouted, then, 'Ili do zavtra!' (*Or until tomorrow!*) We were both laughing. Is this how friendships begin, or do they begin long before their fulfillment, with a small longing for connection on both ends? A small sense that, were we to sit down together, we would connect instantly? I'm still not sure I have it right, still not sure which one moment works like the volta in a sonnet—the moment the speaker's voice or attitude shifts, a sort of poetic tipping point."

When I wrote this, I must have suspected that Anya had become the best friend I'd found during my short time in Columbia. But I couldn't have known, in those early days, that I would call her at 11:30 at night, that she would be the first person I'd tell when Pete decided to take a job back in Chicago, leaving me in Missouri. Or at two in the morning, sobbing and drunk on my front step, pulling up tufts of lawn just to feel something, after Pete broke the news of his yearlong affair, of his decision to leave me. I couldn't have known that one of our first knitting sessions would end with Anya in tears, telling me about an argument with her husband earlier that day. Was one of these the volta?

Or was it the first time we danced, both of us? It was dark already, evening in late March, when I arrived before Anya at an outdoor concert not far from the university campus. I worried I wouldn't spot her amid the crowd. But somehow, too, I knew I would see her—and sure enough, even before the music had begun, she danced up the sidewalk, a lone wave moving across a still sea. Soon the deejay spun quick house beats, for which my coordination was no match. But Anya's face was a permanent smile, her body in perpetual movement. The night was unusually balmy for early spring, and soon Anya had removed her sweatshirt and I my sweater and thick scarf, tossing them down on the ground with a pile of purses and other too-thick outer layers. Anya danced alone, but moving through the crowd, as if dancing with everyone at once. I kept an eye on our purses and sweatshirts.

It made sense: Anya choreographs herself in terms of other people. She is forever entwined with someone. It is a quality I couldn't help but notice because I do the same, placing the people around me—especially female friends—on hierarchies where I am nearly always at the bottom. I admired Anya's ability to embed herself in any group of people without hesitation, to pull them into her perpetual dance. When she spotted a friend from her Indian dance troupe, the two of them moved in immediate synchrony, despite the dissimilarity of this house beat to their traditional Indian Odissi. And when Anya and another friend tried to talk, but strained to hear over the bass and treble, Anya wrapped her arm around the friend's elbow and steered her farther from the stage. When, at the end, her husband arrived and stood next to her, Anya's fingers curled around his and even then, she never stopped dancing.

* * *

I am reminded of this passage by the choreographer Bill T. Jones: "The dancer steps, he pushes the earth away and is in the air. One foot comes down, followed by the other. It's over. We agree, dancer and watcher, to hold on to the illusion that someone flew for a moment." I recited this passage to myself as Pete and I, just days before he left for his "temporary" stay in Chicago, watched one of Anya's less impromptu dance performances. She was in a campus dance troupe, and on this occasion, they were performing a traditional Indian Odissi dance, a tribute to spring. In Indian dance, the dancers do not leap, do not stay suspended for long periods. Rather, they are controlled and grounded, yogalike in their motions. But even in this style, Anna seemed suspended, seemed always to remain in the moment before her feet touched the ground, and I felt us conflate, again, and I knew that was where we were, right then—the two of us, dancers.

* * *

Or perhaps our volta was not when I danced, but when Anya sat still. A few weeks later, late in spring, she and Viktoria had poems to read for a class on Pasternak. Anya hadn't had time to read them, given that she and her husband had been planning for her mother's arrival from St. Petersburg that evening. She ran her fingers through her blonde hair, ruffling it. Her needles and yarn shook in her hands. So as Anya and I knitted, Viktoria began reading aloud from the book of poems. What was not lost on me was that Viktoria was doing this so Anya could get her classwork done and still knit with me—that both she and I saw how important this small part of the week had become for our friend.

Viktoria reads beautifully, slowly and in a quiet voice with a slight Southern (Southern Russian, that is) accent—her voice is as lilting as she is tall and lanky. So we sat there and knitted, Vika reading, and the room felt so calm, the experience so entire, almost too big for the small office.

I don't remember what poem Viktoria was reading at that point, but I like to think it was this one, titled "Zemlya"—"The Earth":

130

Для этого весною ранней
Со мною сходятся друзья,
И наши вечера прощанья,
Пирушки наши завещанья,
Чтоб тайная струя страданья
Согрела холод бытия.

That is why, in early spring,
My friends and I gather there,
And our evenings are farewell wishes,
And our words, final affirmations—
So that the secret spirit of our suffering
Has warmed the cold of our living.

* * *

In the summer, when classes had ended, time had freed up, and Pete had just told me he was leaving me, knitting with Anya kept me afloat, helped me surface from that underwater feeling that consumed me in the first days after finding out about the affair. Anya and I were still both working on the same hats, our progress slowed by final exams and papers, the end of the semester, the end of my marriage. But in summer, knitting became our afternoon ritual, became my only way of moving through those June and July days that would otherwise have languished, too slow, too heavy with mid-Missouri humidity.

Anya and I knitted barefoot on a picnic blanket in the park. We knitted at coffee shops and our favorite café, which has a large patio bathed by afternoon sunlight. We knitted on the sofa in my hot living room, sweaty curls stuck in tendrils to the back of Anya's neck. We knitted poolside at Viktoria's apartment complex, drinking smoothies

Anya made with not much fruit and a lot of vodka. Each afternoon, as we rewound our yarn balls and stowed away our unfinished hats, I would ask Anya when she wanted to meet again, always secretly hoping it would be soon. And always, she would answer as if it were a question: "Zavtra?" *Tomorrow?* She always seemed to hesitate, as if she were asking too much of me. But I now realize that these daily knitting sessions were what got me through that summer, what allowed me to knit away Pete and the past, to let my role as knitting teacher and best friend supplant the role I'd lost as a wife. And I think that Anya, too, came to value them as much as I did. She loved the calm that knitting brought over her, especially as things continued to get worse with her husband. Her mood varied daily, changing with the cycle of fights and reconciliations they seemed confined to. She opened up to me, found a shoulder to lean on at the same time I leaned on her. Our knitting calmed us, and we calmed each other, becoming the confidants we both needed.

And so it was that we met tomorrow after tomorrow, all summer, until finally on one of those tomorrows, an evening sitting on the patio of a local pizza joint, Anya cast off the final stitches of her hat. I showed her how to weave in the tail ends with a darning needle. In spite of ninety-degree weather, she put the hat on and wore it for the rest of the evening, reaching up occasionally to run her fingers over the cashmere stitches, as if to remind herself that it was real.

* * *

Too soon, it was the end of summer. Our hats had been finished for weeks, and Anya had moved on to baby booties for her newborn nephew. After knitting through the late afternoon and well into the evening at our favorite café, she and I were headed to a friend's house for a party. Our walk took us through the campus of the small women's college in town, whose brick buildings are clustered on the northeast edge of downtown. As we walked the diagonal paths that traversed broad, grassy expanses through campus, we heard music—dark chords on an organ. As we neared the small, brick chapel at the heart of the college, the music amplified, leaking louder and louder into the night.

"Let's go in and listen," Anya said to me. Months earlier, I would have hesitated, would have backed away as I had at the square dance, afraid of being the only awkward observers intruding on someone's night music. But now, I didn't. I had become accustomed to Anya's whims, learned to take these moments not just for hers, but for my own.

We tugged at the chapel's stained-glass double doors, but they were locked. We circled the building, tried another set of doors. Those, too, were unbudging. A night watchman, suspicious of our urgency, or perhaps of the fact that we were carrying six-packs of beer to take to the party, approached us. He said that there was a wedding the next day, that perhaps the organist just wanted some last-minute practice.

So Anya and I settled for standing outside. We stood leaning against the chapel doors, pressing our faces against the stained glass, as if willing the music through invisible, unsealed cracks. The song was, we agreed, too elegiac for a wedding. Its low, slow, minor-key chords crept slowly around us. Anya closed her eyes. I looked at her for a moment, then closed mine. And we stayed that way until the music ended, until we opened our eyes and set off, now more slowly, more aware of the streets' summer silence.

* * *

Every time we had these moments, I was compelled to look back to our beginning, as if to see the trajectory of our time together.

I saw Anya's first, stumbling stitches and she heard my first, stumbling words. Before long, we were making hats together. I spoke Russian comfortably and understood even the quick, quiet words Anya and Vika used with each other. I danced. Anya sat still. If nothing else, I came to identify that we were, by summer's end, so far from where we had both started, even if we hadn't yet traversed the whole distance.

Russian has different verbs for different chronologies of motion. The verb for motion that's still happening is different from the verb used to describe motion that happened in the past, that's been completed. There is one verb, *idti*, that can be used only if one is actively on foot at the moment. It would be used, for example, if I were to call Anya as I was walking to meet her. It says, "I'm on my way right now." When I think of my relationship with Anya, it is in terms of this verb. Our motion is still—is always—under way. *My idyom vmeste*—we are in motion together.

WHITE APPLE

Columbia, Missouri, 2011

The only way to know tenderness is to dismantle it.

—Diane Seuss

The summer of 2011, the summer Pete left me for good, I was taking a class on representations of women in Russian film. The class was taught by my favorite professor at the large state university—an Ivy League graduate named Nina, whose quick-witted jabs at students were her way of saying she liked them. She never made fun of me. On account of that, I tried desperately to impress her. I had taken previous classes with her, mainly Russian-language courses, and it seemed she always resisted my overeager attempts to earn her approval: the perpetual raised hand in class, the requests for additional reading, my 100% test average at the end of two semesters. I went to Nina's office hours with pointed questions: how to conjugate some unusual verb, or how to decline the Russian word for "day," which always left me hung up on what's called a "fleeting vowel"—a letter that disappears in certain forms and reappears in others. She would succinctly answer my questions and then ask, "Anything else?"—a quick dismissal. I always wanted to say, "Tell me something about yourself. Tell me how to open you up." But I didn't. In spite of the admiration I harbored for her, I put away my textbook and left. I know now that, like me, she doesn't trust easily. She is slow to open up, having enough times loved the wrong person. And the blame is partly mine: I hadn't opened up to her, either, though I longed for the chance to.

It arrived in that film course, the summer Pete left me. There was something about the nature of a summer-semester class—the languid heat outside, perhaps?—that eased Nina's demeanor. In a lecture hall that our group wasn't large enough to fill, Nina sat at the front atop a small table, her legs swinging as she led our discussions of the filmmakers Dziga Vertov and Mikhail Kalatozov. She had traded in her button-down shirts for shifty cotton dresses, her black leather boots for strappy sandals, pulled her thick blonde bangs off her forehead with a barrette.

One day in class, we watched Kalatozov's *The Cranes Are Flying*, set in World War II Russia. It's the story of two lovers, Boris and Veronika, separated first by war and then, forever, by Boris's death on the battlefield. In the final scene, the widowed Veronika, unable to accept that Boris is dead, arrives to meet him at a homecoming celebration in Moscow. She searches in the crowd in vain, clutching flowers for someone not there to receive them. She is left to look up, where she sees—black against the bright midday sky—the silhouettes of hundreds of cranes, flying.

In the hushed, darkened classroom, I wiped tears from my eyes. Nina got up from her seat in the back row of the lecture hall and flipped on the lights. After she had descended the stairs to the front of the room and turned to face us, we all saw that her eyes were red. She wiped her cheeks with the back of one hand.

"I still can't teach this film without crying," she said, choking on just those few words but laughing at herself, as well. "Go home. Just go home."

Her early dismissal wasn't a mean one, we all knew. Rather, we saw that she couldn't go on, that her crying had broken down the barrier of authority that she put between herself and all of us. Even Nina was vulnerable.

Maybe that's why I approached her after class the next day. Maybe that's why, after we'd discussed the week's readings, I quietly said, "Nina, I'm getting divorced."

"What?" she said. "What happened?" I gave her the quick version as she tucked notes into a file folder: Pete's affair with a friend of ours, revealed a year after it had begun. My question to him: *What has happened between the two of you?* His answer: *Everything.* His hasty move to Chicago to be with his lover, to leave me. It might have been odd to share this out of nowhere, but my life wasn't completely foreign to Nina. After all, she frequently ate at the brewery in town where Pete had been a server. "Oh, he's cute," I remember she'd said when I pointed out that he was my husband. She had seen us together, too, when Pete accompanied me to the Russian-style feast she'd hosted at her small, bungalow-style house the previous spring.

"Come talk to me anytime—if you want to," she said, and I knew she meant it. But I feared seeming too needy. What I've realized since, though, is that Nina *likes* to be needed. We are similar in that way; I've always wanted to be relied upon, rather than to rely on someone else. But Nina was, in her small way, giving me permission to depend on her. I was slow, though, to catch on.

By the next week, when I still hadn't stopped by her office, she repeated her offer as we left class: "Really, I'm here if you need me. And my office hours this afternoon are at Top Ten."

I laughed. Top Ten Wines was a wine shop and bar whose owner was a friend of Nina's. She often stood in when her friend was out of town. So that afternoon, I stopped by on my way home from campus, not sure what to expect from our conversation, but certain she would be hurt if I turned down the same offer twice. I sat at the bar while she sliced cheese and green apples to set out at happy hour. After Pete left, I had no desire to cook for one, and no appetite to justify a full meal. I subsisted that summer on Wheat Thins and white wine. Nina must have known this, because she offered me a small plate of crackers and a glass of pinot grigio as I told her the whole story.

At one point—I don't remember what I'd just said—she set down her knife and turned to me. "I once had a similar thing happen," she said, referring, I guess, to the affair as a whole.

But she let her voice trail off, turned back toward the cutting board, and seemed to dig into the next apple with new ferocity. I continued my story. I wish now that I had seized that moment of opening. I wish I had offered her the same chance she did me: a gentle "Tell me what happened" or "Are you okay, now?" But I didn't.

I just know that when I left, as I was finishing my bottomless glass of wine, which she wouldn't let me pay for, she came around from behind the bar.

"I'm not a hugger," she said. "But after all that, you need a hug." And she quickly wrapped her arms around me, just as quickly pulled back.

In some ways, I suspect it took Pete leaving me for Nina to respect me. In her eyes, now, I was an adult, an equal. My own life, I

saw then, echoed something dark in hers, as if she had once asked the
same question and heard the same response:

What has happened between the two of you?

Everything.

* * *

Nina wasn't even supposed to be my professor. After all, I was
at the large state university to earn a doctorate in English, not to study
Russian. But the classes consumed me, and Nina's contagious enthusiasm
for the language and literature quickly swept me up, finding me spending
more time in the cozy fourth-floor Russian office than in my own dank
basement cubicle at the far edge of campus.

Nonetheless, I harbored a certain fear of Nina. At one point,
I believed I had completely lost her respect. It was a Friday late in the
semester, and we had an exam in Russian-language class that day. I
agonized over these exams, put in hours and hours reciting four-syllable
verbs and obscure nouns, memorizing grammatical structures, and
rewriting my composition for the essay section of the test. At the time,
I thought I did this for my grades, but now I realized how much I did
it to impress Nina. I reveled in getting a test back with "102%" and a
smiley face at the top in her red scrawl.

Even after three or four of these biweekly exams, I still found
myself nervous before each one, arriving fifteen minutes early to class,
shakily setting out two pencils and a large rubber eraser (a necessity) on
my desk, flipping one last time through flashcards whose order I already
knew by heart. Before Nina entered the classroom, a few of us had been
discussing why the last exam's grades, though we'd received our tests
back days ago, still hadn't been credited to us in the online gradebook.
So when Nina came in, I raised my hand and asked her when they

139

would be posted.

Maybe she was already having a bad day. Maybe she had too many papers to grade, too many conference presentations to write. Maybe she had fought with the boyfriend none of us knew she was dating, the one she would marry in just a few months.

"I already said this three times last week," she said. "Because some people retook the exam, I can't post the grades yet." Then, under her breath, she muttered something about having to teach for thirteen weeks straight with no break until Thanksgiving. I see now that her frustration was not directed at me; I simply evoked it. But at the time, I took her harsh words as a personal insult, a sign of what I'd done wrong rather than whatever was going wrong for Nina. I bit my lip, trying not to cry over what I knew should not have made me so upset. But I cried anyway, turning my face over my right shoulder, toward a wall, so the other students wouldn't see. I pulled a tissue from my schoolbag and set it alongside my two pencils and eraser.

* * *

The rest of summer, the summer that Pete left me, brought small moments of opening up. Nina got married, and when I arrived at her reception in a local art gallery, I was surprised to find I'd been the only graduate student invited. I joined her and her husband for dinner and a roller derby bout at the local fairgrounds, where we drank cheap beer and cheered loudly. When I stopped by Top Ten Wines to see her, she introduced me as her friend, rather than her student. But the real moment among them all was when I gave a reading at a local bookstore. Nina showed up.

The small shop was crowded and all the seats taken. Nina stood, leaning gently on a bookshelf behind the rows of chairs. She became my focal point as I read, the face I looked for to calm me every time I glanced up from my manuscript and into the audience. But at some point, she disappeared. She seemed to have leaned herself into the shelf, her face hidden within its wooden frame. I continued looking up in the same direction, a bit distracted, waiting for her to re-emerge. She never did, but after the reading, she came up to me. Her eyes were red.

"You made me cry," she said. "I had to hide."

I wondered what words of mine, exactly, had brought her to tears, where I'd found her soft spot. The piece I'd read was one about Pete and his years-ago German crush, Charlotte. I tried to remember at what point I'd first noticed Nina hiding. Was it at these lines?

Charlotte had the benefit, in her relationship with Pete, that I never would: She and Pete would always be in those first stages of love, doomed—or maybe privileged—to never progress to the mundane. She would always remain enigmatic, to both Pete and me, for what we didn't know about her.

Or these?

Maybe Charlotte, like me, plays with her bottom lip when she's nervous. Maybe she, too, forgets to water houseplants. Maybe she leaves dirty dishes in the sink. But Pete will never know that about her, and as such, she'll always remain a romantic ideal, someone whose image remains untarnished by what happens when we really get to know someone. And I'm still not sure which is better: to know our loves, or to remain in the bliss of not knowing them.

Nina was so new in her love, and I can never know the point that opened her up, that made her turn her face toward the bookcase. I can know only that something in my own relationship with Pete had been the same for Nina, that I had put her experience into words in a way she understood too well. I had realized this about her: that every time I was willing to share my vulnerability, she returned it with hers, with a tenderness that betrayed the stoicism she tried so hard to keep intact.

After the reading, Nina and I lingered. The shopkeepers put out wine and beer, and we sat drinking glasses of cabernet and talking to locals who asked me questions about my writing. Nina listened reverently, her high, easy laugh punctuating our discussion. As I reclined in an armchair, I looked over at her, slightly slouched on a footstool next to me. She brushed her blonde hair away from her face, took another sip of wine, and might have leaned toward me faintly, so little that I didn't then notice.

* * *

It was mid-September, the fall after the summer that Pete left me, and Nina and I had just been to a concert by the band Gomez. She had offered me her extra ticket, aware that Pete and I had just finalized our divorce, that I was in need of a distraction. We'd danced and talked our way through the show, lingered afterward over glasses of wine at a nearby bar.

Then, loath to go home, we stopped at the steps in front of the white-pillared Baptist church on Broadway. When we sat down, there, knees pulled to our chests in the fall-night cold, the air turned clearer. I saw her in a way I had not allowed myself, before. Here, on these steps, on this unexpected, headlong night, she was no longer just my professor, and more than just my friend. It was as if, upon our sitting, she simply transformed. She was suddenly beautiful in a way I'd seen but not acknowledged, the chin-length blonde hair, the blue eyes slightly shy behind her glasses.

She put her hand to my cheek, let it linger there.

"You're lovely," she said. It ended the guilty surge of this mistake, my piece-by-piece dismantling of her façade.

Hidden in our spot behind a row of street-parked cars, we kissed.

After we had pulled apart not quickly enough, I leaned into her and pressed my face into her collarbone. And I stayed there, dangerously comfortable, could've slept there, especially when she leaned her head down so it rested atop mine. I laced my fingers through her hair, which was smooth and thick and straight. I like to imagine that she twirled one of my long, brown curls around her index finger, let it fall back to my shoulder. We stayed that way, me leaned into her, her head on mine, and said nothing, as if justifying to ourselves the very moment we were in.

* * *

This, this telling, is my way of reliving and relishing that night, the one I know will never happen again. I know because she told me this. I went into her office a few days later, not intending to talk about us—intending, instead, to talk about another professor who'd unexpectedly left the department, about the readings for our upcoming class, about everything but us. It had been my way of re-establishing our relationship as professional, or maybe of verifying that it still could be professional. But after we discussed everything else, she looked me straight in the eye.

"I don't know what to say about Tuesday," she said.

"I don't, either," I responded.

I didn't have the nerve to tell her that I had been replaying that kiss in my head for three days. I didn't tell her that I could remember her slight hesitance subside and something else take over, something of her that was willing to surrender to the moment, to be dismantled. But that nonetheless, this wasn't what I'd been hoping for, in all my openings up to her. As hard as I tried not to, I could still feel her tongue on mine. And her soft shoulder, how it felt like such a resting place. I told her instead what I did know, that this was risky for her. She had much more at stake than I did: her job, tenure. But I knew it wasn't this that was holding her back. It was what we both hadn't mentioned. Finally, she did:

"I have a new husband," she said, "and I love him."

Still, I saw how, in our next Russian drama seminar, she seemed to teach directly to me, her eye contact somehow more persistent than usual. And she had brought me a book, Pushkin's collected prose.

"I had two copies," she said, as if to justify the gift. I walked home cradling it after class that night, whispering lines to myself that I barely could make out under the dim streetlamps.

* * *

As Nina and I had left the Gomez concert—in early fall after the summer Pete left me—and before we ended the night with a glass of wine at that nearby bar, before we began the morning's first hours on the church steps, I had seen a poster in the theater window advertising another show in just a couple of weeks.

"Blind Pilot!" I said, probably too loudly. I must have grabbed Nina's arm, taken her by the elbow in my excitement. "We have to go. I'll buy us tickets."

I knew that it wouldn't be an easy show for me. Months earlier, Pete and I had stopped for an afternoon drink at a divey little bar a few blocks from home. As Pete conversed with the bartender about bicycle repair, I let my attention wander to the music playing on the sound system.

"Who is this?" I'd asked, compelled by the driving melodies, the soaring horns.

"Blind Pilot," the bartender said.

It's hard for me now to listen to the music Pete and I shared, that we discovered together and turned into the soundtrack of us. I will never, I suspect, return to Lyle Lovett, whose outdoor concert at Ravinia we attended four summers straight. Emmylou Harris, too, is impossible, given the endless string of her CDs that Pete burned and sent to me—with custom sleeves he'd designed—while he was in architecture school in Chicago and I lived in Oregon. Leonard Cohen, though I have returned to his music, brings me a nostalgic sort of torment, as does Mahler's First Symphony. It was what Pete would put on his stereo in our first days together, its first and second movements our learning each other's bodies by night, its low and slow third movement lulling us to sleep.

I have realized now, though, that the memories I associate with those songs can be replaced. I can superimpose upon the music a new association. For Blind Pilot, it was Nina. I burned her their CDs, brought them awkwardly to her office hours. And for the two weeks leading up to the concert, I walked to and from campus every day playing their two albums on my headphones, my pace quickened by the music. I mouthed along with the lyrics and, walking home from bars late at night, reveled in singing along quietly as I cut through darkened, empty parking lots—the ones where Pete once held my hand. My favorite song—one I had just discovered on the newer of the two albums—was "White Apple," and I played it on repeat, immersed in its chorus: *So if I haunt you, if I do, if my shadow leans up on you, too, no good intentions or ways I talk. I'll just leave a light lit for you to walk.* More than wanting Pete's hand, now, in these parking lots, I thought of Nina, wondered how this next concert could possibly live up to its prelude.

* * *

The night of the Blind Pilot show, a Monday, Nina and I had our evening Russian drama course. I lingered afterward in the small, hushed seminar room tucked in a corner of the fourth floor. Nina answered other students' few questions, and I felt guilty for lurking. It seemed as if our leaving together would betray something in our relationship that had transcended student and professor, as if there was a necessary covertness in hiding our unprofessionalism. If the other students gave us odd looks as we descended three flights of stairs together, I didn't notice, but still, I felt guilty. Neither Nina nor I mentioned our excitement about the concert until we were both outside the building, in the safety of early fall rain, walking to her car.

I secretly wondered whether these concerts were our excuse for playing out something even more covert, whether she was waiting for the dim light and the low hum to bring us together in a way that could be achieved only in moments of music and revelry. We were both quiet in her car on the short drive to the concert, as if only the time spent standing too close in a crowded theater could bring out what we really had to say—or didn't have to say, at all—to each other.

The theater was already packed when we arrived, and we nudged our way as far forward as we could get. When the music started, we sang along and danced, clutching beers. We stood too close, shoulders brushing. Here, here, were the memories of Pete replaced: the driving melodies, the soaring horns, the words that I'd applied to one relationship now cast upon another. When the band began the first chords of "White Apple," I felt Nina glance over at me, as if checking

146

to see whether I would cry. I wouldn't. I would sing and sway and let the song take on new meaning, a meaning not sad for what I'd lost but filled with the possibility of what I knew I couldn't long for, but did, nonetheless: *This faint sweetness, this wick of light, this white apple full of bites. A white apple full of what has slipped away from me; full of flesh sweet as memory; full of hope grown from a fallen tree.*

At the show's end, the crowd cheered the musicians back onstage for an encore. But the band did something unusual: They hoisted the upright bass down off the stage, into the crowd. The guitarist and banjo player hopped down with their instruments, too. The guitarist urged the audience to gather around and sing along. The three musicians began to play, and as if by instinct—for we all knew the words to the title track from their first album—the crowd sang along. *They're playin' our song. Can you see the lights? Can you hear the hum of our song? I hope they get it right. I hope we dance tonight before we get it wrong.*

Nina and I were pressed up close against each other, just a few feet from the band and surrounded by the crowd. And somewhere during the course of that first verse, she took my hand in hers. And we stayed that way for the rest of the song. We sang with everyone else, but sometimes, I caught her voice rising above the others and it was all I heard. It was the perfect gesture, that covert hand-holding that no one but us knew about, the crowd so dense and the lights so low. And it was perfect because it had a necessary end: The song would stop, we would have to applaud.

After the show, I walked with Nina to her car, the rain unrelenting, the air damp and clammy, the streetlights made somehow brighter in the haze.

"Do you want to go somewhere and get a drink?" I asked her. It was my move, my gesture toward the coda—music's added ending—that we'd had last time. But I now see that it was foolish. The concrete church steps were wet, so we couldn't sit. The air too cold, even with our knees tucked to our chests, even with our heads leaned into the other's, for us to ever be warm.

"I'd love to, but I should go home," she said. What she didn't say was what we were both thinking: that this night could not end up like the last, but that we'd had our moment, pressed together by the crowd, overwhelmed by the low bass hum and the slight sweating of each other's palms. I recognized that Nina's hand-holding was her way of saying that we couldn't be, yet feelings lingered. In that moment, I relished the possibility of more of these nights, the thrill of the music overshadowed by the thrill of small moments of indiscretion.

After she offered me a ride home that I declined, I walked to the nearby bar, the same one where she and I had gone, together, after the previous concert. The place was nearly empty, save for a few students hunched over laptops, their faces eerily illuminated against the dim late-night light. I took my seat at the bar, the one where I'd sat last time, next to where Nina had sat. I ordered a glass of pinot grigio and sipped it, silently and alone.

I walked home listening to Blind Pilot, barely noticing the rain, not bothering to open my umbrella. The streetlights seemed to have dimmed again, the air to have grown warmer, more foggy. Mist rose from the sidewalks and empty streets, from the black expanse of the parking lot I traversed. I couldn't hear the night—the likely hum of distant traffic on Interstate 70, the last few revelers calling out to each other as they left downtown bars, the sounds of a city shutting down—over the music turned up loud. I couldn't even hear myself as I sang along: *I wandered home saying your name.*

* * *

My friendship with Nina, to this day, remains tinged with the slightly metallic taste of the unattainable. The better I get to know her, the more our interactions are shaded by a longing that I've given up trying to conceal when we're together. On one such January evening, we met up at a local bar to have a glass of wine and catch up after the month-long winter break. I talked about how the break, which I'd spent in Prague, had left me more wistful than ever over Pete. There was something about not just the emotional distance but its geographic equivalent—thousands of miles, an ocean—that exacerbated my sadness, that made him feel more gone than ever.

I did not tell Nina that I had felt the same about her, that I had wished for her presence as much as Pete's in the cobblestone streets. I did not tell her that for the one postcard I sent her, I had drafted many more and tucked them away carefully in the side pocket of my backpack. I did not tell her about the musings that peppered my notebook, the one I took with me to small cafés where I nursed a glass of wine: *What is the word for a professor and her student kissing on the steps of a downtown church at 3 a.m., awash in quiet and the late fall moon? It is something that must remain unspoken, nameless, as if by putting language to it, we might hold it too still.*

Pete's departure freed me to see the light change on the haystacks around me, to dwell on that night with Nina, that one romantic moment, whereas before, I would have been unable to occupy my desire for her—a desire I harbor, still, a desire to return to those church steps, to woodsmoke in the air, to those golden leaves about to die and drop.

As I thought of this new yearning but spoke, instead, of Pete, Nina propped her elbows up on the polished wood bar and rested her chin in her hands. The chunky pewter bracelet she always wears slid down on her arm.

"But you know," she said, "once you're over this, you'll want it back. You'll want the pain, just to feel anything."

And she was right. It was better for me to harbor my longing than to feel nothing at all. This, after all, is how we move on: We replace one longing with another. Nina knew that. What she didn't know was that my new longing belonged to her.

WHAT'S LEFT UNFINISHED

Columbia, Missouri, 2014

In my house, now, there is a mid-century modern dresser that was once my grandma's—it sat in her craft room and stored tidy rows of embroidery floss and balled-up yarn remnants. Under my care, the dresser has a drawer dedicated to various sewing supplies—spare buttons, fusible interfacing, and embroidery hoops; another that holds wrapping paper, gift bags, and spools of ribbon; and a drawer of projects my grandmother did not finish before she died—crocheted squares that need to be connected into an afghan, half of a quilted Christmas tree skirt. It also contains a drawer of Pete's gifts to me, for my want of anyplace else to put them.

Our relationship could be traced by the gifts we'd made for each other, always at holidays, eschewing effortless store-bought goods in favor of arts and crafts. Of course, we both enjoyed the making as much as the giving. In fact, I wonder, now, whether our ritual making of these gifts wasn't more selfish than we realized at the time. Which was greater, I still can't say: my own pleasure in the making, or the pleasure I felt in handing over my gifts to Pete.

Of course, the process of making is a contemplative one, in which I lose sense of time and self, and fall into a meditative state induced by the repetition of stitches or pencil strokes. But making gifts also allowed me to picture Pete's and my future together, how he would use the gifts I was making, or how we would use them together. I now see that many of my gifts were, in fact, gifts for us both. From fabric printed with green apples, I sewed us a set of placemats with pockets for utensils. These could be rolled up and tied with grosgrain ribbon, for easy transport to picnics, though I don't recall us ever using them. One winter, I knit Pete a blanket from bulky-weight wool yarn in variegated shades of gray and brown. My yarn choice, however, was a poor one; for when we began to use the blanket, it shed terribly, leaving our clothes covered in lint. The blanket was quickly retired, and thereafter, lay draped over the back of our sofa—its only value aesthetic, not functional.

Pete's early gifts to me were always songs. The first of these, I lost in one of my many moves, but not intentionally. He had written the song out on music-score paper, and I had that as a reminder of the real gift: Pete had taken me, at night, into the hushed music building on Northwestern's campus, which by day rang with the sounds of students practicing all types of instruments in small, sealed rooms. But at night, the cacophony was gone, the building lights dimmed. Pete sat on the bench before a grand piano and played for me my birthday song, a song whose score I can't now consult, but I remember that it depended on the piano's low notes, on Pete's prolonged keystrokes.

The second song Pete wrote for me is titled "Portrait of a Rain-Soaked Moment." It's an homage to a morning when I'd been in Chicago on one of the many visits I made to him from San Francisco after I had graduated. I was staying with him in the Andersonville neighborhood, on the north side of Chicago, where he lived in a dilapidated house with four college friends. We'd awoken early one morning and decided to take a sunny-day drive to our favorite brunch spot—Tre Kronor, a Swedish restaurant that served up overloaded omelets and plate-sized cinnamon rolls. It wasn't far away, just up Foster Street past the Swedish Covenant Hospital and North Park University, an idyllic drive through the far edges of the city, where the streets were tree-lined and the sidewalks wide and clean. But while we ate breakfast, the weather changed abruptly. Dark clouds rolled in, and though we made a run for it, trying to reach Pete's car before the storm came, we were too late. We gave in to the rain, slowing our run to a walk, holding hands as our clothes soaked through. We climbed into the car, shivering, and Pete turned on the heater to warm us. At the time, we still knew how to move slowly together, how to walk in the rain and enjoy it, merely because the other was present. The song Pete wrote changes from fast to slow: hurry to quiet resignation, the pleasure of existing in a moment rather than trying to outrun it. We were, after all, young and naïve, not yet encumbered by the worries of graduate school or our careers—concerns that, over time, would accumulate and pry us away from each other, both geographically and emotionally.

In the months between my visit and Christmas, Pete had written this song and turned it into a work of art. He glued the musical score onto a red cloth backing and framed it with Plexiglas and strips of beveled wood. He painted the wood in a gradient of colors: red to yellow, green to indigo blue, using oil paint—a choice I would not have made, for oil paint will warp wood over time. But I did not tell him that when I accepted the gift on Christmas Day, nor when I took it back to San Francisco and hung it on the wall of my studio apartment. After that, the song would hang on the walls of our first Chicago apartment together, and then above my bed in Oregon, and then in Chicago again, where we lived after we were married. The only place it would not be displayed was in the small, white Missouri house. We never got around to hanging it, I guess, before Pete left.

Pete gave me other gifts, as well: a handmade vase built with glued-together cardboard and a test tube, to hold a single flower stem; a small collection of poems, printed on pocket-sized, colorful cardboard; a pencil drawing of me on cardstock of the slightest green hue. I reciprocated with my own gifts for Pete: a picnic quilt with ties and handles for easy portability to the many outdoor concerts we attended, a pair of knit socks, hand-bound books of my favorite poems, the trunk I'd refinished to preserve my countless letters to him. I wonder, now, whether the presents I gave Pete have met a fate similar to those he gave me. One by one, I've ushered them all into a drawer, where they are out of sight but not quite forgotten. I'm not sure whether I could permanently get rid of them. How would I, anyway? I wouldn't have the heart to throw them in the trash. But to donate them to Goodwill is also an absurd proposition—for who would understand the sentimental value of these otherwise useless objects? What are our gifts fated to, after the relationship that inspired them is gone? I ask myself this whenever I open the drawers of my bureau, reminded of gifts that have been given to me but are now stashed away, gifts that my grandmother intended to give but did not have time to finish. I am more compelled by the secrets inherent in my grandmother's gifts: Whom were they for? How would she have finished them?

My grandmother died just a week after Pete's and my divorce was made official. My dad called me late one evening to tell me she had fallen ill and been hospitalized. Her decline had been quick, unexpected; the very day she had collapsed, she and my aunt, my dad's sister, had been looking at new assisted living facilities she might move into. She'd been on her feet one moment and curled up on the floor the next, my dad told me. I packed a bag and set out early the next morning for the seven-hour drive to Indianapolis. In my car, parked in the hospital garage, I carefully slipped my wedding ring back on my left hand. This was hardly the time, after all, to break the news to aunts and uncles, and especially to my grandmother.

She lay in bed looking pale, an oxygen mask strapped to her face, her hair neat as always, pincurls still in place. Someone had brought her magazines from the hospital gift shop: *Better Homes and Gardens, Martha Stewart Living.* I sat on the bed next to her and we paged through the magazines, pointing out decorative touches we liked in the photos of staged houses. She must have missed her house, then, its curved staircase with sturdy wooden balusters, the stained glass in the front window, the plush blue carpet so thick and soft underfoot. I missed her house, too, and I wondered what no one said: Had she seen it for the last time? Would she not ever return? I wonder, now, whether my question was selfish; for if she would not return to the house, nor could I return and find her there, whistling in the kitchen, spreading thick swathes of butter on the toast she always made for me after I'd spent the night there. The last time I'd visited, Pete had accompanied me. We spent the night in Lisa's Room, where I used to read on the window seat. We awoke to the smell of bacon, eggs, toast, and coffee, which my grandma had prepared while we'd slept in, comfortable under heaps of homemade quilts in the four-poster bed. It was the last time my grandma would see Pete.

At the hospital, she inquired about him as we paged through the magazines. She did not ask, "Where is Pete?"—her polite demeanor not implicating him in his absence—but rather, "How is Pete?" The question was, of course, inevitable. But I wonder, now, whether she sensed my hesitation in responding, saw how my eyes must have lowered, or heard my voice soften.

"He's good," I answered. "Very busy with work. He's sorry he can't be here."

I'm convinced, now, that my grandmother knew. Perhaps she could not have guessed the extent of our separation, or about Pete's affair, or the fact that the divorce was already final. But in some way, a way that depends on my grandma's ability to hear my unspoken thoughts, as she always had been able to, I believe that my grandma knew.

For my grandmother's funeral, in Gas City, Indiana, just blocks away from the house where she had lived for more than fifty years, my aunt urged all of us to return with the items she had made for us. My mother brought the mauve dress my sister had worn as Uncle Jerry's flower girl. She laid out my christening gown, crocheted from fine white yarn. There were brightly colored striped sweaters my cousins had worn as children, quilts pieced by hand, and many pastel baby blankets. We draped the blankets over the backs of the sofas that lined the funeral parlor, and my aunt carefully arrayed the clothes on tables set up for just that purpose.

"It looks like a rummage sale," Uncle Jerry had said, trying to elicit a smile.

Indeed, if one stepped back a bit from the circumstances, it could have been. But I liked the homage to all the gifts my grandma had given us, all the care and time that she had dedicated to her crafts. Did she know, I wonder now, that everyone had saved her gifts for all these years, despite the fact that some were outgrown or no longer used?

* * *

While I try to finish my grandma's ungiven gifts where she left off, and while I try to discern what she had intended, I let Pete's presents fall into disrepair. The rubber cement that held together his cardboard vase has lost its grip, so it now sits in four pieces in the top drawer of my dresser. The song he wrote me and framed by hand has also come apart, the backing pulling away, the painted wood warped and unglued. It seems a shame to throw these items away. Pete did, after all, put so much effort into them. And I see no harm in having reminders of the fact that we once were in love, that these gifts were not intended to evoke the removal I feel now. But maybe that's when gifts should be thrown away or given away: when they no longer elicit the feelings they were intended to. These gifts, after all, are about decoration more than utility. And laid away in a drawer, they don't even serve their decorative purpose. They are merely clutter, I suppose, remnants of a life, foregone.

With my grandma's gifts, I take utmost care. My intention is not to finish them for myself, but rather, to consider who their intended recipients might have been. Perhaps most troubling is the collection of crocheted granny squares, clearly intended to become a blanket, but for whom? They are beautifully made—simple off-white squares, but in the center of each is an elaborate pink rose with green leaves. I don't know how to crochet, despite my knitting skills, and will have to learn how in order to join the squares into a blanket. I have not yet tried, for I fear ruining them, even though I know their construction is sound.

Instead, I have completed the smaller, simpler projects first. I've begun seaming the Christmas tree skirt by hand, a project I work on a bit at a time while I watch movies in the evenings, thinking of my grandmother doing the same in her rocking chair, watching reruns of *The Lawrence Welk Show*—the only television I recall her enjoying. I have finished just one of her projects: a small lace doily.

The doily had been stored with my grandma's usual care: in a plastic Ziploc bag along with the yarn and crochet hook she had used to made it. Like the unfinished afghan, it was a set of granny squares still unattached. But these were more intricate, still: lace, crocheted with fine, white thread on a hook no thicker than a toothpick. There were ten of them in all, and I fretted over how they should be arranged. Finally, I settled on a rectangle two squares tall and five wide. Their bound-off edges were straight and firm, with well-defined crochet loops where I knew I'd need to run the thread. I knew how to do a simple whipstitch through these loops, and so I threaded my embroidery needle with a long piece of the cotton thread my grandma had thoughtfully enclosed with the project. The stitches were so tiny and so many that each square took hours to join to the neighboring one. I could only connect one at a sitting before my hands cramped up and my eyes ached from strain. Yet this was the simplest part of the project. My grandma, even with arthritis that pained her in her last years, had managed to crochet the intricate lace that made the project beautiful. Finishing is the easy business, I thought, as I admired the time, the skill, and the patience my grandmother had devoted to making a single doily, a decoration that might go unnoticed in most homes—including my dad's. I knew that this would be a Christmas gift for him. For though he's not necessarily one to appreciate a doily—or anything that might be construed as clutter—I knew he would value it because it had been started by his mother and finished by his daughter.

I imagined a place for it on his narrow entryway table, which also held the flag, folded into a triangular frame, that had been draped over his father's coffin. His parents, now, were memorialized on this table, represented by the objects they'd left behind, objects that stood in for them. Perhaps it's that notion that motivates us when others die and we are left behind: We feel a duty to continue where they left off, to complete what's been left unfinished. For as I seamed the doily, I imagined my grandma's hands where mine now were, thought of my last day with her, holding hands in her hospital bed. Over all the years and all the skills she taught me—a keen sense for thread tension, for holding the needle loosely—perhaps she had seen the day coming when she would leave projects behind. And she hoped that my hands would remember hers over mine, guiding my slender fingers in the ability to finish what she had not been able to, herself.

I wished, in that moment, that I could whistle as my grandmother had when she worked—in the kitchen, at her sewing table. But I can't whistle, no matter how I purse my lips or with how much force I exhale. There is just the sound of my own air, escaping. That is how, with each breath, the body does its own math, which depends only upon subtraction.

HAYSTACKS, REVISITED

Santa Fe, New Mexico, 2018

The light in New Mexico in August is high and blinding, and I-25 shimmers as my car ascends Glorieta Pass, just outside Santa Fe. When I drive through northern New Mexico, I marvel at the towering rocks, how they tell time that spans eons. Some layers glow golden in the sun, others gleam red—strata carved by melting ice, by receding water. I'm headed to my friend Kristin's to housesit while she goes on a hiking trip. I don't know it yet, but this will be the closest I've come to calling New Mexico home. For three years, since taking a teaching job here after my PhD, I have bounced around rental units—hard to come by in my small town at the base of the Sangre de Cristo mountains. I am relieved to leave behind my two-room studio with peeling linoleum and arrive at Kristin's spacious adobe with brick floors and wooden ceiling beams, a backyard garden and two talkative sister cats.

Even though I'll be there for just two weeks, I quickly empty my suitcase and hang my clothes in the closet space Kristin has cleared out for me. I position my laptop on Kristin's desk, in her art-filled office, imagine myself writing where she, too, writes. I go to the grocery and buy ingredients for the meals I'll cook in her spacious kitchen, put them away in the pantry and refrigerator.

Right behind the house is a trailhead, and every morning, I awaken in the cold and still-dark to run along the Santa Fe River, which isn't a river at all, but instead, a dry arroyo through which a river only occasionally flows. For a few weeks each year, I'll later learn, water is released into the riverbed to preserve its path, to reinvigorate its muscle-memory of carving through dry land. This practice clears the way for the river's sporadic natural formation, brought on by late-summer rains. Just a week earlier, in fact, part of Kristin's fence had been toppled when storms poured down and the river—perhaps having forgotten its path—jumped the banks.

Alongside detritus from the storm, overturned logs and leaning trees, I run west to the edge of town, past the horse corrals and vacant lots set off by corrugated aluminum fences. Then I turn back east and run toward the mountains, purple with the sun rising behind them, rays long and languorous like the days I will spend here. My sense of direction is now calibrated to this landscape, to the rustle of chamisa, to the southerly winds that summon the rain, to the way oblique sunbeams fall not between tall buildings but over mountains.

A tree in Kristin's backyard drops peaches by the dozen. Each day, I crouch on the ground, holding a colander, and pick up the fallen fruit, sometimes bruised or pecked open by birds, but fine for making tart filling or jam. Then, the way Kristin showed me before leaving, I test the peaches still on the tree to check their ripeness. They're ready, she said, when they give a little under your touch, when you can indent them with your thumb. I load a colander full and carry more, still, in the hem of my shirt. Inside, the peaches gleam on the kitchen counter, holding dew in their furry skins.

Tomato vines with thick, sturdy stems use the peach tree as their trellis, climbing skyward though they're laden with deep-orange fruit. These, too, I pluck from their plants and carry indoors, placing them in a bowl next to the peaches. I marvel at the simple industry of taking care of Kristin's garden, though I know I'm capable only because my time there is temporary. Two weeks is surely not enough time to kill this garden.

Staying in a friend's house feels like an act of intimacy. When Kristin and I had met a year earlier, I'd quickly admired her green eyes, her elegant hands, her spiky blonde hair, her ability to speak the truth gently. We bonded over the shared labor of book manuscripts, went to concerts in Santa Fe's Railyard district, drank morning tea on the patio of her favorite café. If I said I was never attracted to her, I'd be lying.

The things in her house, though, were a window to days before I'd known her. I studied the titles on her bookshelves, discovered her propensity for saving empty yogurt containers, marveled at oil paint-ings, masks, and sculptures—which no doubt had stories of their own. Much of what I knew of Kristin's story came from her published essays about gender-queerness, anorexia, and wildlife advocacy. Living in her house, though, felt like an essay in objects—each of which hinted at something I didn't know about her.

* * *

She had learned my past life earlier in the summer, when she had been invited to read at a literature festival in Chicago. Knowing

I'd once called the city home, she asked me along. The return was a bittersweet one, for I'd been back to Chicago only a couple of times since that last visit to Pete—the one after he told me what had happened. The one after I heard "everything" as his answer. After those two days awash in blue.

Despite my claims to know Chicago well, my sense of direction had disappeared. "We need to walk north," I'd tell Kristin, accidentally walking south, instead. She corrected me for our five days there, her internal compass already calibrated to the city—Lake Michigan to the east and straight, sprawling avenues headed west.

On our first day there, Kristin and I wandered the downtown streets, which were brighter than I remembered, with slanted sunbeams falling between tall buildings. We strolled along the turquoise shore of Lake Michigan, the breeze brisk and the water dotted with far-off boats. At lunchtime, I suggested we go to one of my favorite places along the Magnificent Mile: a little Italian deli that served savory paninis stacked with prosciutto and dripping melted mozzarella. But when we arrived at the spot where I'd had so many lunches, it was now a Starbucks, green-lady logo mocking my attempt at return. This was no longer my city.

It didn't feel like Pete's city, either, even though I knew it was—knew that at any moment I could turn a corner and find him in the shadow of a skyscraper. I no longer felt his presence there, no longer associated memories of us with the many places Kristin and I visited. Too much had changed. As I'd learned in Prague years before, tracing memories of my visit there—tracing memories of my love for Pete—we can never return to a city and see it the same way. No experience is replicable, even in the same place. Returning to Chicago eight years after I'd lived there reinforced the impossibility of anything remaining the same. I felt as if Chicago was a place entirely new and unfamiliar, and I no longer the person who had once occupied it.

When a city changes around us, we're less likely to notice that it has changed, at all. It is harder to perceive what happens gradually—the accumulation of wrinkles on a lover's face, the winding of rivers over time, the way our own bodies age. Imagine if we could step away from these things, if we could leave them and come back, so that we could see how different things indeed are, what eight years can do.

* * *

Ravinia, an amphitheater on Chicago's north shore, was for me, as Amy Lowell wrote, "the smell of all summers": lakewater and damp grass, citronella candles, picnic blankets freshly washed after months stowed away, Off! bug spray. It was there that Pete and I had lain on the broad lawn and listened to Mahler's symphonies, had held each other while Lyle Lovett crooned with the crickets, had danced barefoot among fireflies to Emmylou Harris. Perhaps trying to summon my nostalgia for the place, I'd suggested to Kristin that we go to a Friday-night piano concert, Schumann and Chopin. But even in June, the balmy days of the Midwest summer hadn't yet arrived in Chicago. Kristin and I found ourselves woefully unprepared for the cold that night. The evening was pallid, overcast, starless. We ignored the chill, spreading a blanket on the grass, opening a bottle of wine and drinking it from plastic cups. The sun fell yellow. The air turned colder, still. Kristin shivered and curled into herself, folding in half. We shifted under the blanket, doing our best to cover ourselves. So chilly and damp was the weather, in fact, that the pianist had been moved indoors, his music piped out to the lawn by a sound system.

Kristin turned to me during intermission and asked how the book was going. I must have shrugged. For at the time, I knew it wasn't

164

done, but couldn't have said why. She asked, then, the question I knew I'd been avoiding: "Do you admit in it that you cheated on Pete with women?"

It was obvious to me that she had figured out the story I'd been trying to tell all along—what my own memoir was saying that I hadn't acknowledged. I hadn't even known what I was revealing. Yet in those knitted gifts, hands on hips, and quick kisses, there was not only hidden the romance I wanted, but also the reason I was as guilty as Pete for his leaving.

My feelings for women had, in fact, dwelled in me since long before Pete had left, since long before we'd even met, though I hadn't felt I could confess that—to Pete or in my writing. I had to sustain my attempts to make Pete seem like the one who'd left, though of course, I was equally guilty. In her memoir, *The Way We Weren't*, Jill Talbot writes, "Whether it was in her Jeep or out the door or with a bottle, she was always leaving him. But when she writes, he's the character who leaves. So she has written a forgiveness, given her character a trait she never possessed. One of loving someone with abandon." I did not love Pete with abandon. Instead, I loved him with abandonment.

I'd come out shortly after moving to New Mexico, so Kristin had known me only as gay. But I see now what she could: the difference between the "I" of my essays and the "I" writing now. What seemed a continuum of change to me must have looked like stark contrast to her. Only now, with the benefit of hindsight and the geographic distance that separates me from many of the women I wrote about, can I see what love I put into making gifts for them, what love I put into writing about them—because I didn't feel I could love them out loud. In all of the ways I was creating for them, I was expressing what I felt I couldn't, otherwise. I recall moments when that act of creating felt like a transgression, when I felt that if Pete knew my intentions, he would be more than slightly jealous of the feelings that underpinned the giving, the writing, the time spent pining over women. Indeed, though, time changes what feels true, just as surely as it shapes city skylines and rivers shape the terrain, just as surely as light changes, falling on haystacks.

* * *

Kristin knew my history with Pete, knew about the haystacks, so she didn't react with surprise when I said I wanted to go to the Art Institute. Our first stop was, of course, the Impressionist wing. I had told her about the haystacks, though it was Georges Seurat's pointillism she wanted to see. I did not remember the collections being so vast, and as we strolled through labyrinthine rooms of Van Goghs, past Degas and Renoir, I wondered whether the haystacks had been taken down. Surely, we would have found them by now. At last, through the doorway to yet another room, I spotted Monet's water lilies—a harbinger of the haystacks that might be nearby. I tugged Kristin by the arm—"This way," I said, my sense of direction back intact for a moment. We stood before the haystacks. I did not weep. For this time, they did not look bleak. Even the washed-out whites and ivories of winter hay were saturated, multi-textured, full of life in their own pale way. And what if the sun on the other, brighter bundles was not setting, but rising? What if the blazing oranges and pale pinks signaled a new day, not a dying one?

We exited the Impressionists through broad glass double doors that opened out to that large, marble staircase. We descended. Of course, this was the moment I had sought all along—to go back down those marble stairs, a reversal of my climbing them years before in search of Pete's favorite paintings. A walking away.

I saw in that moment my own transformation—from disliking the haystacks to appreciating their embodiment of my own change. I had gone from straight and married to gay and single, and was now standing in front of these paintings with another queer woman. I understood my need to love women in a way would be reciprocated, not just as friendship, but romantically. I acknowledged all the women I'd loved but could not reach for. As I moved in to see Monet's brushstrokes up close, I saw that I was the artist of Pete's departure. Pete deserved to leave me, though he may not have known to how great an extent. We both knew we were growing apart, but he was the only one willing to make the call, to reveal his secret as I could not reveal mine.

Despite quick trysts and kisses with women in the days before and during Pete, it wouldn't be until I was thirty-six that I'd go on my first "real" lesbian date. She was sporty and smart, witty and impatient, a Libra. I fell in love with her immediately, and with abandon. I kept the lease on my small-town apartment but moved into her Albuquerque house. After just a week together, as we were standing in her kitchen and starting to make dinner, she told me to close my eyes and hold out my hands. Into my open palm, she pressed something cold and small. I opened my eyes to a pewter charm embossed with the word "love." I tucked it into my pocket. When she broke up with me after four months, I was more devastated than I had been by Pete's affair, by our divorce. Days when I think of her are still awash in blue. I confess, the charm still lives, now, in my wallet, a reminder that I was once loved in the way I had so long sought: by a woman.

That relationship, of course, is not what this book is about. But still, I have to ask myself, is this book not about what I thought it was? Is it not, in fact, about how Pete left me, but rather, why? I struggle to discern whether the love I *write* for Pete is stronger than the love I *felt* for Pete. Perhaps my writing about him is an atonement—for I have written him a love I never completely had. I've been inclined to write about his absences, his transgressions, all the while omitting my own. This is what Kristin meant, I see now, when she asked me on that cold Ravinia night how this book could be true if it didn't extend to the present, if it didn't acknowledge my own culpability. But the present requires confessing that I am as much to blame as Pete for his leaving.

Talbot, in *The Way We Weren't*, admits that the story we tell is malleable, that the truth is mercurial. Yet she keeps plugging away, watching the truth change with each draft, each version that brings her up to the present. "Change the story, and everything changes," she writes. "My mind went back to scenes from the months surrounding his leaving that had confused me, and I could now read them through this new point of view." Indeed, I feel at last that I have arrived at the point where I must interrogate myself as a narrator. After all, the undertones of romance are not as subtle as I had thought. The writing betrays a secret I convinced myself I was keeping, a destination I yearned for without knowing, at the time, what it was.

* * *

On my last night at Kristin's, before I return to my small town, before school starts in just a couple of days, I walk to the park behind her house, the same place I get on the running trail each morning. I cross the wood-plank footbridge that takes me over the arroyo, still empty save for strewn sticks and stones, the occasional plastic bottle. I sit on a concrete bench and watch clouds swell overhead. Late summer in New Mexico is called "monsoon season" for the rains that roll in most afternoons, sometimes persisting into the evening. Not a drop has fallen here, but the shape of the clouds tells me there's rain to the east, the kind of hard, permeating rain people pray for in these parts. I watch the sky cycle through shades of blue—colors with illustrious names like *cerulean* and *indigo*—until there is no word left for how dark they are.

Then I hear it: the sound of rushing water, the sound of a river. It's swept down from the mountains, pressing through the arroyo with urgency, taking along with it the bottles and the stones and the sticks, straining at its banks, glittering in the moon-sliver. I watch the river make itself, watch it flow under the footbridge, growing higher. I watch a swath of water wind its way through the earth, on a path it carved so long ago, yearning for a destination only it can know.

WORKS CONSULTED

Atwood, Margaret. "Hair Jewellery," in *Dancing Girls and Other Stories*.

Blind Pilot. "3 Rounds and a Sound."

---. "Oviedo."

---. "White Apple."

Cohen, Leonard. "Chelsea Hotel No. 2."

Didion, Joan. "The White Album," in *The White Album*.

Elephant Revival. "Feathers Rise."

Gioia, Dana. "Summer Storm," in *Interrogations at Noon*.

Iglesias, Enrique. "Escape."

Jones, Bill T. *Last Night on Earth*.

Kundera, Milan. *The Unbearable Lightness of Being*.

Lowell, Amy. "Aubade," in *Amy Lowell: Selected Poems*.

Monet, Claude. *Haystacks*.

Once, dir. John Carney. 2007.

Pasternak, Boris. "Земля" ["The Earth"].

Riley, James Whitcomb. "Little Orphan Annie," in *The Best of James Whitcomb Riley*.

Seuss, Diane. "White violet, not so much an image," in *Four-Legged Girl*.

Strand, Mark. "Coming to This," in *Selected Poems*.

Talbot, Jill. *The Way We Weren't*.

Tedeschi, Susan. "Don't Think Twice, It's Alright."

Treasured Chests. "Antique Doll Trunks." *Antique Trunk Restoration, Sales, and Research*. www.oldtrunks.com/doll-trunks/

Wilder, Laura Ingalls. *Little House on the Prairie*.

Yeats, William Butler. "The Lake Isle of Innisfree," in *The Collected Poems of W. B. Yeats*.

ACKNOWLEDGMENTS

I first want to gratefully acknowledge the literary journals that published chapters from this book: *First Inkling*, "By Being Written, They Would Disappear" (Pushcart Prize nominee); *poemmemoirstory*, "My Hands, Remembering"; *Post Road*, "Haystacks"; and the *South Loop Review*, "The Chipp Inn."

I owe a multitude of thanks to those who guided me toward creative nonfiction and helped me take the first steps toward thinking of myself as a writer. Ann Hagedorn, Marjorie Sandor, Tracy Daugherty, Maureen Stanton, E.J. Levy, and Julija Šukys led insightful workshops and devoted close attention to my manuscripts in their early stages. Even though she's not a creative writer, but rather, a Russian professor and now associate dean, I owe so much of my success to Nicole Monnier, who showed me what it looks like to really love teaching, and who collaborated with me when I was a mere graduate student to help me pursue my love of studying (and composing) endings. All of you modeled for me how to write, to teach, to pass along what we love.

I'm grateful to my MFA colleagues at Oregon State University, especially Claire Carpenter and Isabelle Brock, for the sense of camaraderie and community you fostered. I also owe thanks to all in my workshops at the University of Missouri, who provided sound advice on earlier versions of this memoir. Joanna Eleftheriou, my deskmate, conference-travel companion, and fellow memoirist, deserves especial thanks for providing lentil soup and a listening ear during the toughest times chronicled in this book. My colleagues and professors in the Russian master's program at the University of Missouri offered a warm, welcome reprieve in Strickland Hall, and I'm grateful to each of you for your friendship and intellectual discourse.

Moving forward, I look at where I am now: New Mexico Highlands University, where my colleagues in the English department and across the university have offered unwavering support. My senior colleagues Peter Buchanan, Juan Gallegos, Brandon Kempner, Eddie Tafoya, and Donna Woodford-Gormley have been instrumental in their support of this memoir. I also want to thank Tyler Mills for our weekend writing sessions that resulted in so much inspiration and so many wonderful conversations about writing and teaching. I would be remiss to end this tribute to Highlands without thanking my students, who, each and every one of you, have made me a better educator and person.

My family has supported me all the way as a writer. One weekend, years ago, my dad and Uncle Jerry visited Chicago to attend a Northwestern-versus-Indiana football game with me. Afterward, we went to a Wrigleyville bar, near my apartment. My uncle, hearing of my aspirations to write, said to me, "You have a story to tell, and you should tell it." That was long before I knew what the story was. My parents, Grandma Fath, and my aunts, uncles, and cousins have been unflagging supporters of my career and my dreams. Thank you all for your unconditional love.

I am so fortunate to have two writer friends who have generously read early drafts of this memoir and provided valuable suggestions. Kristin Barendsen is not only a writer and editor extraordinaire and an astute reader of my work. She's also an incredibly generous friend and has been by my side through whatever life has thrown me these past few years. I'm so grateful to her for introducing me to a group of lovely friends in Santa Fe. Kristin is the reason this memoir doesn't actually end where it ends; I value the memories we'll continue to create, even before they've unfolded. I'm grateful also to Kristi Markey for her wisdom as a reader of my work, as well as for our literary conversations and time spent reading out loud to each other.

Finally, I want to thank Femi Sobowale and Zac Furlough of Passengers Press for their wonderful guidance and advice through the editing and publishing processes. Thank you for taking a chance on this manuscript so many years in the making. I felt from the outset of our discussions that Femi really understood my intentions for this book, and I'm so grateful for their integrity, kindness, and editorial rigor. *My Hands, Remembering* could not have found a better home than Passengers Press, and I'm indebted to both Femi and Zac for ushering it into the world.

As I write this last section, I'm evacuated from my house due to wildfires in northern New Mexico, the place where my story ends, for now. May this land continue to nourish us, and may we nourish it in the aftermath of its burning—a lesson for how we might live in reciprocity with the places and people that dwell around and within us.

[c|mp]

PROUD MEMBER OF THE COMMUNITY OF LITERARY MAGAZINES AND PRESSES